Racial Discrimination

Series Editor: Cara Acred

Volume 236

Independence Educational Publishers

First published by Independence Educational Publishers

The Studio, High Green

Great Shelford

Cambridge CB22 5EG

England

© Independence 2013

British Library Cataloguing in Publication Data

Racial discrimination. -- (Issues ; v. 236)

1. Racism -- Great Britain. 2. Great Britain -- Race relations. 3. Great Britain -- Ethnic relations.

I. Series II. Acred, Cara.

305.8'00941-dc23

ISBN-13: 9781 86168 634 3

Printed in Great Britain

MWL Print Group Ltd

Contents

Chapter 1: Racial discrimination

What is race discrimination? 1

Racial prejudice 3

Growing up with racism in Britain 6

Race in Britain 2012: Has life changed for ethnic minorities? 8

Spotlight on racial violence: January – June 2012 13

Islamophobia filtering into classrooms 15

Racism in the classroom 16

Integration in England today 17

White people paid more and ethnic pay gap widening 18

Race to the top: the experiences of black students in higher education 19

A test for racial discrimination, findings 20

Racism and discrimination against gypsies and travellers 21

Caught in the headlines 22

Chapter 2: Debating discrimination

Time to hold the media to account for Islamophobia 23

Prioritise the right battle first: not Islamophobia, but racism 25

Met chief: 'I can't be sure we're not institutionally racist' 26

Police racism: 293 cases, five dismissals 27

Confronting indirect racism 28

Can you excuse casual racism? 29

Online racism 31

Jail for student in Muamba Twitter race rant a perversion of justice 31

Are East Europeans victims of racism in the UK? 32

One in three Brits admits they are racist 33

Blackness is not a costume 34

Free speech: Are we getting the balance right? 35

A message from British National Party leader Nick Griffin MEP 37

Racism kicked out of football? Not yet 38

Tottenham defend fans over Society of Black Lawyers threat 39

Key facts 40

Glossary 41

Assignments 42

Index 43

Acknowledgements 44

Introduction

Racial Discrimination is Volume 236 in the **ISSUES** series. The aim of the series is to offer current, diverse information about important issues in our world, from a UK perspective.

ABOUT RACIAL DISCRIMINATION

The UK is often hailed as a place of tolerance, acceptance and multiculturalism but, in a recent poll, one in three Brits admitted that they are racist. What is racial discrimination? Are we a nation too concerned with being 'politically correct'? What about free speech? This book explores the current landscape of racism in the UK, and goes on to debate the issues associated with discrimination. Should we concentrate less on the idea of Islamophobia and more on racism as a whole? Is it ever okay to tell racist jokes? What is being done to tackle racism in football? These ideas, and many others, are discussed within.

OUR SOURCES

Titles in the **ISSUES** series are designed to function as educational resource books, providing a balanced overview of a specific subject.

The information in our books is comprised of facts, articles and opinions from many different sources, including:

- Newspaper reports and opinion pieces

- Website fact sheets

- Magazine and journal articles

- Statistics and surveys

- Government reports

- Literature from special interest groups

A NOTE ON CRITICAL EVALUATION

Because the information reprinted here is from a number of different sources, readers should bear in mind the origin of the text and whether the source is likely to have a particular bias when presenting information (or when conducting their research). It is hoped that, as you read about the many aspects of the issues explored in this book, you will critically evaluate the information presented.

It is important that you decide whether you are being presented with facts or opinions. Does the writer give a biased or unbiased report? If an opinion is being expressed, do you agree with the writer? Is there potential bias to the 'facts' or statistics behind an article?

ASSIGNMENTS

In the back of this book, you will find a selection of assignments designed to help you engage with the articles you have been reading and to explore your own opinions. Some tasks will take longer than others and there is a mixture of design, writing and research based activities that you can complete alone or in a group.

FURTHER RESEARCH

At the end of each article we have listed its source and a website that you can visit if you would like to conduct your own research. Please remember to critically evaluate any sources that you consult and consider whether the information you are viewing is accurate and unbiased.

What is race discrimination?

Information from the Equality and Human Rights Commission.

The 1976 Race Relations Act is concerned with people's actions and the effects of their actions, not their opinions or beliefs. Racial discrimination is not the same as racial prejudice. It is not necessary to prove that the other person intended to discriminate against you: you only have to show that you received less favourable treatment as a result of what they did.

Under the Race Relations Act, it is unlawful for a person to discriminate on racial grounds against another person. The Act defines racial grounds as including race, colour, nationality or ethnic or national origins.

To bring a case under the Race Relations Act, you have to show you have been discriminated against in one or more ways that are unlawful under the Act.

Your protection under the Race Relations Act 1976

The Race Relations Act protects you from racial discrimination in most, but not all, situations. You will therefore have to show that the discrimination you have suffered comes within the areas covered by the Act.

On 2 April 2001, amendments to the Race Relations Act came into force which covers public authorities that had previously been exempt. This means that around 45,000 public authorities in the UK are now required to meet the general duty to promote race equality. A few public authorities are exempt, such as the Security Service.

Racial discrimination may occur in the way that someone provides you with goods, facilities and services, including housing. It can also occur in public services, such as health and education and other public services. Racial discrimination may also occur in, the field of employment. There are a few small number of areas not covered by the Act.

The Race Relations Act 1976 (Statutory Duties) Order 2001 identifies specific steps to be taken by public authorities to comply with this specific duty. Discrimination in any of the areas listed in 'What forms does racial discrimination take?' is unlawful under the Race Relations Act.

What forms does racial discrimination take?

There are four main types of racial discrimination: direct, indirect, victimisation and harassment.

Direct racial discrimination

This occurs when you are able to show that you have been treated less favourably on racial grounds than others in similar circumstances. To prove this, it will help if you can give an example of someone from a different racial group who, in similar circumstances, has been, or would have been, treated more favourably than you. Racist abuse and harassment are forms of direct discrimination.

Example: Racial groups

BBC v Souster [2001] IRLR 150

Mr Souster, a presenter for BBC Scotland's *Rugby Special,* complained that he had lost his job because he was English and the BBC wanted a Scottish person. Mr Souster claimed that being English was a matter of national origins, while the BBC argued that, since both the Scots and the English share a British passport, there could be no unlawful discrimination between different parts of the one nation. The Scottish Court of Session, which had to decide whether the RRA applies to discrimination between the Scots and the English, ruled that national origins should be interpreted more broadly and flexibly than just by reference to a passport. As England and Scotland were once separate nations, the English and the Scots have separate national origins and therefore the RRA does cover discrimination between them.

On the question of whether the English and Scots are part of a 'racial group', the Court of Session followed the House of Lords' ruling in an earlier case (Mandla v Dowell-Lee, 1983 IRLR 209), to the effect that '...it is possible for a person to fall into a particular racial group either by birth or by adherence'. The court also observed that, if the way the discriminator treats someone is based on her or his perception of that person's national or ethnic origins, then their actual origins, let alone their passport nationality, are irrelevant.

This definition of racial grounds clearly takes into account the complex reality of national identity, where a person may change their nationality by marriage or geographical migration or indeed simply by association, as well as the complexity of racial prejudice, where a person who discriminates may do so in complete ignorance of the victim's actual nationality or national background.

Indirect racial discrimination

Indirect racial discrimination may fall into one of two categories depending on the racial grounds of discrimination. The first is on grounds of colour or nationality, under the original definition in the Race Relations Act.

The second is on grounds of race, ethnic or national origin. This was introduced by the Race Relations Act (Amendment) Regulations 2003 to comply with the EC Race Directive.

Example: Indirect discrimination

Aina v Employment Service [2002] DCLD 103D

A Black African employee applied for the post of equal opportunities manager in his organisation. He was assessed as having the skills and ability for the job. However, his application was rejected because, unknown to him, the post was open only to permanent staff at higher grades than his. Monitoring data showed that the organisation had no permanent Black African employees at the grades in question.

The employment tribunal held that there was no justification for the requirement, and that it amounted to indirect discrimination on racial grounds.

On grounds of colour or nationality

This occurs when an apparently non-discriminatory requirement or condition which applies equally to everyone:

⇨ can only be met by a considerably smaller proportion of people from a particular racial group

⇨ which is to the detriment of a person from that group because he or she cannot meet it

⇨ the requirement or condition cannot be justified on non-racial grounds.

For example

A rule that employees or pupils must not wear headgear could exclude Sikh men and boys who wear a turban, or Jewish men or boys who wear a yarmulke, in accordance with practice within their racial group.

On grounds of race, ethnic or national origin

This occurs when a provision, criterion or practice which, on the face of it, has nothing to do with race and is applied equally to everyone:

⇨ puts or would put people of the same race or ethnic or national origins at a particular disadvantage when compared with others

⇨ puts a person of that race or ethnic or national origin at that disadvantage

⇨ cannot be shown to be a proportionate means of achieving a legitimate aim.

The definition of indirect discrimination on the grounds of race, ethnic or national origin is in general terms broader than on the grounds of colour or nationality and as a result it may be easier to establish racial discrimination than previously on that ground.

Victimisation

This has a special legal meaning under the Race Relations Act. It occurs if you are treated less favourably than others in the same circumstances because you have complained about racial discrimination, or supported someone else who has. A complaint of racial discrimination means that someone has:

⇨ brought proceedings under the Race Relations Act against the discriminator or anyone else

⇨ given evidence or informatio in connection with proceeding brought by another perso under the Race Relations Act

⇨ done anything under the Rac Relations Act or with referenc to it

⇨ alleged that a person has acte in a way which would breac the Race Relations Act.

The complaint does not need t expressly claim discriminatio when making the complaint.

Harassment

The definition of harassmer introduced by the Rac Relations Act 1976 (Amendmen Regulations 2003 applies whe the discrimination is on grounds c race or ethnic or national origin: but not colour or nationality Harassment on grounds of colou or nationality amounts to les favourable treatment and may b unlawful direct discrimination.

A person harasses another o grounds of race or ethnic c national origins when he or sh engages in unwanted conduct tha has the purpose or effect of:

⇨ violating that other person' dignity; or

⇨ creating an intimidating c hostile, degrading, humiliatin or offensive environment fo them.

Example: Harassment

Anisetti v Tokyo-Mitsubishi International plc Case No. 6002429/98

The Indian-born head of cred derivatives at an internationa Japanese bank in London resigned claiming he had been made to fee like a 'second-class citizen' by hi Japanese employers. He said h had been humiliated, excluded b workers speaking Japanese an underpaid, simply because he wa not Japanese. The bank argue that it was 'natural' for Japanes staff to use their own languag among themselves.

An employment tribunal uphel the complainant's claim that h

had been discriminated against unlawfully, not because of his Indian national origins, but because he was not Japanese. The tribunal noted that the bank had maintained a practice which had effectively excluded the complainant from various activities, and treated him less favourably than others. The complainant was awarded around £1 million in compensation.

Harassment is unlawful not only in the context of employment, but also within:

⇨ partnerships

⇨ trade unions

⇨ qualifying authorities

⇨ vocational training; and

⇨ employment agencies.

It is also an unlawful form of discrimination in education, planning, within public authorities, in the provision of goods, facilities, services and premises, and in relation to the training and

employment of barristers and advocates.

⇨ The above information is reprinted with kind permission from the Commission for Equality and Human Rights, known as the Equality and Human Rights Commission ('the EHRC'). Please visit www.equalityhumanrights.com.

Racial prejudice

An extract from the Communities and Local Government report Race, Religion and Equalities: A report on the 2009-2010 Citizenship Survey.

Perceptions of racial prejudice

3.1 Survey respondents were asked whether they thought there was more, less, or about the same level of racial prejudice in Britain today as there was five years ago. People who said that there was either more or less racial prejudice were asked a follow-up question to determine which ethnic groups they thought faced more or less prejudice.

Headline and trend

3.2 Just under half (47%) of people thought that there was more racial prejudice today than there was five years ago, which represented a decrease on 2008-09 levels when 50% of people believed this. Conversely, there was an increase in those believing levels of racial prejudice had remained the same (from 28% to 32%). It is interesting to note that the proportion of people who believed there was more racial prejudice over the

previous five years was the same as the proportion of people believing there was more religious prejudice over this period (46%).

3.3 Between 2001 and 2007-08, the proportion of people who believed that racial prejudice had increased rose from 43% to 56%. However, the 2009-10 figure indicated a declining trend in levels of perception of increased racial prejudice since 2007-08, from 56% to 47%. The decrease observed between 2007-08 and 2009-10 was compensated for by a rise in the proportion who said there was 'about the same' level of racial prejudice as there was five years ago (from 25% in 2007-08 to 32% in 2009-10). These changes mirror those observed on perceptions of religious prejudice (Figure 3.1).

Perceptions of change in racial prejudice by ethnicity

3.4 As in previous years, White people were considerably more likely than other ethnic groups to consider that racial prejudice had increased over the previous five years. 50% of White people believed this compared with 31%

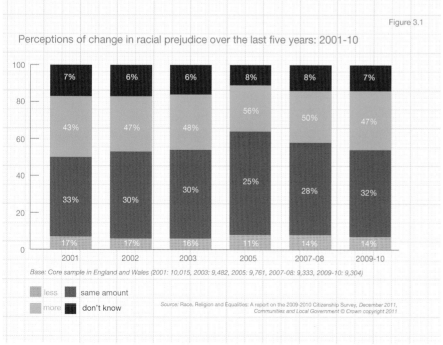

Figure 3.1

Perceptions of change in racial prejudice over the last five years: 2001-10

Base: Core sample in England and Wales (2001: 10,015, 2003: 9,482, 2005: 9,761, 2007-08: 9,333, 2009-10: 9,304)

less | same amount
more | don't know

Source: Race, Religion and Equalities: A report on the 2009-2010 Citizenship Survey, December 2011, Communities and Local Government © Crown copyright 2011

of Mixed Race people, 28% of Asian people, 22% of Black people and 19% of people in the 'Chinese or Other' category.

3.5 Reflecting the overall trend, between 2008-09 and 2009-10 there were falls in the proportions of White, Asian, and Chinese or Other ethnic groups who believed that racial prejudice had increased. However, the proportion of Black and mixed race people who thought that racial prejudice had increased was unchanged.

3.6 The overall trend over time on this measure, as described in paragraph 3.3 above, was also reflected amongst White and Asian people, where the proportion who thought racial prejudice had increased rose between 2001 and 2007-08, and then fell between 2007-08 and 2009-10. The longer term time trend in views among other ethnic groups was less clear cut, although there were consistent falls between 2007-08 and 2009-10 among all ethnic groups with the exception of mixed race people[1] (Figure 3.2).

Perceptions of change in racial prejudice by age, country of birth, gender and ethno-religious group

3.7 As in previous years, perceptions of an increase in racial prejudice:

⇨ rose by age from 37% of those aged 16-29 thinking racial prejudice was higher, rising to 48% of 30-49 year olds, and 53% of those aged 50 or above;

⇨ were higher among those born in the UK (51%) than those born outside the UK (26%);

⇨ were higher among females (49%) compared with males (45%);

⇨ were higher among Christian people (50%) than among Muslim people (29%), Hindu

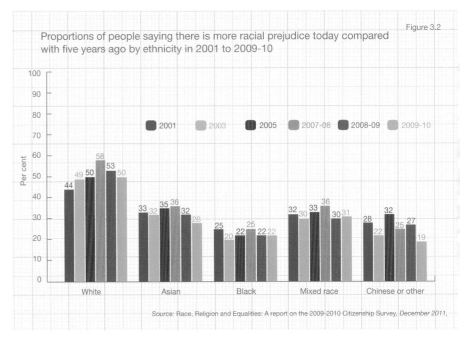

Figure 3.2

Proportions of people saying there is more racial prejudice today compared with five years ago by ethnicity in 2001 to 2009-10

Legend: ■ 2001　▨ 2003　■ 2005　▨ 2007-08　■ 2008-09　▨ 2009-10

Source: Race, Religion and Equalities: A report on the 2009-2010 Citizenship Survey, December 2011;

Indian people (25%), Sikh Indian people (28%) and those from 'other' ethno-religious groups (37%).

Groups perceived to be experiencing more racial prejudice

3.8 People who thought there was more racial prejudice today than there was five years ago were asked which groups they felt there was more prejudice against. As in 2008-09, the three groups mentioned most frequently by those who believed there was an increase in racial prejudice were Muslim people (cited by 38% of people); Asian people (cited by 32%); and Eastern Europeans (cited by 27%).[2]

3.9 Whilst respectively 38%, 32% and 27% of people who believed that racial prejudice had increased respectively cited Muslims, Asian people and Eastern Europeans as being the subject of increased prejudice, the proportion of all people who believed that these groups had been the target of increased racial prejudice were:

Muslims (17%), Asian people (15%) and East Europeans (12%).[3]

3.10 Between 2008-09 and 2009-10, there were decreases in the proportions of all people believing the following groups to be the subject of increased prejudice: Asian people (from 19% to 15%); Eastern Europeans (from 16% to 12%); and Black people (from 10% to 6%). Conversely, an increase was observed in the proportion of all people believing asylum seekers/refugees to be the subject of increased racial prejudice (from 6% to 8%), whilst those citing 'new immigrants' remained unchanged at 8%. There were no changes in the levels citing other groups including Muslims.

3.11 Mirroring the overall trend for perceptions of increased racial prejudice (paragraph 3.3) there was a rising trend between 2005 and 2007-08 in mentions by all people of Muslims, Eastern Europeans, new immigrants and Black people, followed by a declining trend between 2007-08 and 2009-10 among all groups with the exception of asylum seekers/ refugees (Figure 3.3).

[1] The observed fall between 2007-08 and 2009-10 for mixed race people was not significant due to low sample bases.

[2] People were not given any prompts, to avoid leading their answers, and interviewers coded their responses into a concealed on-screen list. This list of groups was designed to cover the wide range of answers obtained, and so includes racial and religious groups, as well as generic groups such as 'new immigrants' and 'Eastern Europeans'.

[3] Calculating the figure based on the total sample differs from the approach in previous reports which only looked at the proportion based on all who felt there was increased prejudice, as quoted in paragraph 3.8. However, the revised approach used here enables trends to be viewed more accurately, and the larger sample sizes allow changes over time to be detected with greater precision.

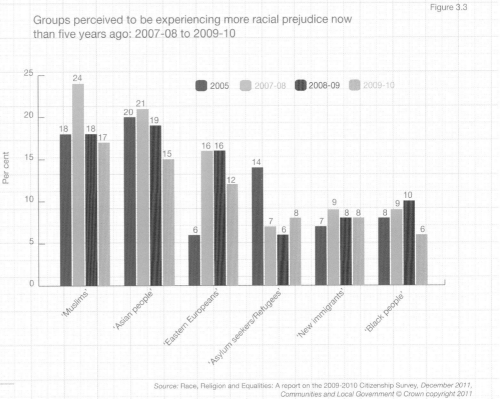

3.12 Looking at the extent to which different ethnic groups cited particular groups as experiencing increased racial prejudice, there were some clear variations. Muslim and Asian people tended to be the groups most commonly cited by all of the main ethnic groups. However, Eastern Europeans were particularly highlighted by White people (13%), and Black people were most likely to cite Black people as subject to increased racial prejudice (9%).[4]

As with religious prejudice, racial prejudice was more likely to be perceived as increasing by White people than people from other ethnic groups, although the decline in this view over time was reflected across nearly all ethnic groups.

Muslims, Asian people and Eastern Europeans continued to be the groups highlighted most frequently as the target of increased racial prejudice, although the overall proportion of people who cited these groups fell between 2007-08 and 2009-10, in line with the wider trend.

21 December 2011

⇨ Information from Communities and Local Government. Please visit www.communities.gov.uk

Conclusions

The longer-term trend data reveal a pattern of rise and fall in perceptions of racial prejudice, with opinions of prejudice rising between 2001 and 2007-08 to reach a peak before falling away again between 2007-08 and 2009-10. In 2009-10, just under half of the population regarded racial prejudice to have increased over the previous five years.

Changes in perceptions of racial prejudice between 2007-08 and 2009-10 mirrored those observed in perceptions of religious prejudice, suggesting this may be part of a broader shift in perceptions about prejudice.

4 The difference between the proportion of Mixed Race people and White people mentioning Black people is not significant.

Figure 3.3

Groups perceived to be experiencing more racial prejudice now than five years ago: 2007-08 to 2009-10

Per cent

Legend: 2005, 2007-08, 2008-09, 2009-10

'Muslims': 18, 24, 18, 17
'Asian people': 20, 21, 19, 15
'Eastern Europeans': 6, 16, 16, 12
'Asylum seekers/Refugees': 14, 7, 6, 8
'New immigrants': 7, 9, 8, 8
'Black people': 8, 9, 10, 6

Source: Race, Religion and Equalities: A report on the 2009-2010 Citizenship Survey, December 2011, Communities and Local Government © Crown copyright 2011

Growing up with racism in Britain

The threat posed by racists on the streets and fascists at the ballot box shows that racism has not gone away. Weyman Bennett and Assed Baig discuss their experience of racism and how to fight back.

'We cannot let history repeat itself'
– Weyman Bennett

Over the last 30 years we have witnessed enormous changes in racism in Britain. When I was growing up in the late 1970s racism was deeply enshrined. At school one of our arts and crafts teachers had two canes. One was black and the other white, and he would use the appropriate one according to the race of the child he was chastising. I am glad to say we broke into the cupboard where he stored the canes and demolished them in an act of revenge.

That act was a consequence of the fight against racism which dominated much of the 1970s and early 1980s. The question of whether black people were here to stay in Britain had not been fully answered, and Britain changed from a country with a labour shortage to one with mass unemployment.

Today racism is no longer seen as respectable, unlike in the 1950s when people openly claimed that black and Asian people were naturally inferior. In a recent opinion poll only 20 per cent of people said that they were prejudiced – a substantial fall. It is important to identify what has changed and the role that integration in schools and workplaces, along with the challenge to racism from trade unions, has played in this.

Now we can see the emphasis shifting from race to religion. This is most noticeable with the rise of Islamophobia. Fascist organisations like the BNP even claim they are not racist, though of course their practice exposes the reality.

Racist and fascist organisations suffered severe defeats in the 1970s and 1980s. The NF, the biggest fascist organisation in Europe, was smashed by the Anti-Nazi League and consistent anti-racist struggles. The old biological concepts of racism were partially demolished, so today the targets of anti-immigrant hostility are not necessarily black and those engaged in racism towards Muslims are not automatically hostile to all black Britons. Organisations like the English Defence League (EDL) are willing to accept black and Asian individuals so long as they accept racism towards Muslims.

Islamophobia remains the cutting edge of racism. In 2001 riots provoked by fascists in Oldham, Burnley, Bradford and elsewhere indicated this new chapter. The New Labour Government narrative tried to explain the riots in terms of cultural separation, not deprivation, and this developed into a full-blown attack on multiculturalism. The 'war on terror' then further intensified Islamophobia.

The gap between the new racism and previous manifestations of racism shouldn't be exaggerated. It is not an accident that less than a month after the 7 July 2005 bombings in London, black teenager Anthony Walker was murdered in Liverpool because he had a white girlfriend.

People from black and Asian groups are around four times more likely to be unemployed than the white population, despite them having the required skills and qualifications. Poverty rates for ethnic minorities in Britain stand at 40 per cent – double the figure for white British people.

Black Power

In the 1960s and 1970s the consequences of the Black Power movement meant that many people blamed the system for producing inequality. Today many Afro-Caribbeans look instead to blame models of family for gun and knife crime, for example. This means the problems are internalised into the black community rather than being seen as rooted in wider society against which we can struggle collectively. This can change, especially against the background of government spending cuts which will affect all groups.

When racist organisations such as the EDL or the BNP have taken to the streets they have been met by overwhelming united resistance by black, white and Asian people. It is this spirit and tradition of an integrated working class that can determine our future.

One of the most convincing factors in my journey to becoming a revolutionary was the experience of unity in the working class. In the aftermath of the Great Miners' Strike in 1985 there had been rioting in Tottenham, north London, and Winston Silcott was falsely accused of killing PC Keith Blakelock. The newspapers were full of lurid racist stories. But visiting miners' villages to raise support for the defence campaign I witnessed magnificent solidarity. George, Winston's brother, received standing ovations in working men's clubs. Impoverished miners dug deep to give money to the campaign. The riots were seen as class riots against a vicious Tory government and the miners felt solidarity for others they identified as being the same as them.

I was at Hull University then, where there were only three black students, but one thing was absolutely clear to me: socialists were at the forefront of the fight against racism. They occupied banks against apartheid and faced expulsion to stop Enoch Powell coming to our college. I joined them because they were the tribunes of the oppressed but they also had a vision of a world free of racism and oppression. I have never regretted that decision.

Today the growing tide of Islamophobia is reminiscent of the anti-Semitism of the 1930s. We cannot let history repeat itself. The historic coming together of the TUC, the Muslim Council of Britain and hundreds of other organisations for the national Unite Against Fascism demonstration in London on 6 November is a vital chance to derail the racists and the Nazis. We must seize the time to shape the future.

Weyman Bennett is joint convenor of Unite Against Fascism and a leading member of the Socialist Workers Party.

'We need resistance on all fronts' – Assed Baig

On my first day of secondary school, as I walked through a narrow alleyway between the two school sites used by all the students, an older boy saw me and shouted, 'Paki bashing!' He grabbed my head and smashed it against the wooden fence. Distraught and shocked, I saw the head teacher moments later and told him what happened. He told me to come see him later. I did. Nothing happened.

My father had decided to send me to this school because it was majority white. His colonial thinking made him believe that a majority white school would mean a better education for his son and therefore a better chance in life. There were only 12 Asians in the first year. It was acceptable to call people 'Pakis' or 'bud bud ding' and say we smelt of curry. At first I responded to it aggressively – when I was physically attacked I would fight back. This landed me in trouble and I soon found myself on my last warning before I would be suspended. My father, a traditionally strict Kashmiri man, gave me a stark warning: if I was suspended I would be in serious trouble. I could no longer fight back. I still remember the times I was punched in the face, while being called a Paki, and not fighting back out of fear of my father.

Every day we would receive racist abuse. We even used to have a 'Paki bashing' day – you can imagine what that entailed. But we were let down by the authorities, and the only time the racism stopped was when we stood up for ourselves. However, the school authorities did not see our actions as a reaction to racism and sometimes we were treated more harshly than those subjecting us to the racism.

Nothing has changed. The police and government do not see the difference between self-defence and racism. Now when we face up to the EDL we are treated the same as them, when there is a major difference.

This indifference comes from a lack of understanding about racism, oppression and the rights of communities to defend themselves or, even worse, a complete lack of empathy with those communities. I believe the police and government do understand, but they just see anti-racists as the problem. The idea goes that if people do not protest then the racists will just go away. This kind of thinking leads to mass oppression and tyranny.

There are also among us black and Asian people who have been bought up in a generation who have lived sheltered lives, who have gone to posh schools and whose education has made them look down on their fellow brothers and sisters. So when Asians defend their streets from fascist thugs they are condemned because they make 'us' look bad. When Asians stand up to people calling them Pakis, they are told not to demonstrate as it only makes it worse.

Since 2001 the atmosphere has got worse. Never have I felt so discriminated against, so frustrated and not a part of society: stopped at airports, stared at in train stations and, once again, subjected to people who feel that they can use racist and Islamophobic language, because now it seems like it is backed by the state. When Jack Straw made his comments about the Muslim face veil, immediately I felt the backlash on the streets of Stoke. People drove past shouting 'Paki!' Muslims were the centre of attention once again. It has been intense, frustrating and very upsetting. I got rid of my television because I could not bear to watch the news – every day it would be Muslim bashing. There was nowhere to run or hide.

I have debated with racists before. They did not call me Paki but covered their racism in pretentious language. But debating with them gave them the idea that their argument was legitimate. The jokes at school had started with curry, corner shops and taking the piss out of our names; it ended with Paki bashing. We stopped it not by debating, or depending on an establishment that would rather the problem went away – we stopped it

by standing up to it and hitting back. Hitting back did not defeat racism. It defeated the violent racist. We need resistance on all fronts; we need to tackle the root causes of racism. This is not done by giving a platform to fascists or condemning those who defend themselves from fascists.

My experiences are not the worst, by any means. I do not want people to feel sorry for me, nor do I want pity. I want people to understand that our experiences shape us and that if you are black or Asian your experiences are going to be very different.

Every time I thought it was too much, I was lucky enough to have the solidarity of comrades in the movement who helped me through – people who stood up to racism and fascism, who stood up to Islamophobia, against war and against the scapegoating of the Muslim community. The effect is immense. When Muslims see white people standing shoulder to shoulder with them and speaking out, it gives them confidence to come out and have their voice heard.

Nothing demonstrates this better than the demonstration in

Birmingham against the EDL. Most of the Muslim youth had never been on a demonstration before, but when they saw white, black and Asian people standing up with them the experience left an indelible mark. Wherever the EDL turn up they are faced with local Asians and anti-fascists. This is down to the solidarity the movement has shown to the Muslim community. The only way that we can defeat racism in the future is to once again create an atmosphere where Islamophobia and the new language of racism are deemed unacceptable in wider society.

Assed Baig is an activist and journalist.

October 2010

⇨ The above information is reprinted with kind permission from the *Socialist Review*. Please visit www.socialistreview.org.uk for further information.

Race in Britain 2012: Has life changed for ethnic minorities?

Some things have improved for the black and Asian communities since the murder of Stephen Lawrence in 1993, but Britain still has a long way to go before it can call itself a colour-blind country.

Last week, as Gary Dobson and David Norris's 19-year escape from justice finally came to an end, the distraught parents of another young ethnic minority man visited the scene of their son's death.

Anuj Bidve, a 23-year-old Lancaster University student who was shot dead on Boxing Day, was killed for the apparent crime of not being white.

Nearly two decades after the murder of Stephen Lawrence, has anything changed? And what is life really like for young black and ethnic minority people in Britain today?

In the high-visibility worlds of the establishment, entertainment and sport, there are signs of progress: there are more than four times as many black and ethnic minority MPs in Parliament as there were in 1993. A Muslim woman takes her seat at the cabinet table every Tuesday. An African-born man is in charge of a FTSE 100 company. Black and Asian actors regularly take leading roles in prime-time TV series.

The population has changed since 1993: then ethnic minorities accounted for 5.1 per cent in England and Wales; the latest figure is 8.7 per cent.

Some would argue that the major dividing line in Britain today is not race but class, and that Stephen's killing captured the nation's interest only because he was from a 'nice' middle-class family and had aspirations to be an architect.

But the statistics for ethnic minorities are bleak: black men are 26 times more likely than their white counterparts to be stopped and searched by police, while black men and women in their early twenties are twice as likely to be not in employment, education or training as white people. And black and Asian defendants are still more

Last Tuesday, despite a plea from Stephen's mother Doreen not to rejoice, there appeared to be collective back-patting when Norris and Dobson were found guilty, as if the verdicts had cleansed Britain of racism.

Yet reminders of racial hatred were never far away. Yesterday, Subhash and Yogini Bidve, having flown to Salford to visit the scene of his kiling, were back in Pune for his cremation. Mourners watched a flower-filled open coffin carried through the streets.

There is nothing that can comfort them in their loss. But perhaps the prominent coverage of Anuj's death, and the impact the Lawrence trial has had, show that one thing has changed for the better since 1993, and that is ultimately because of one young man from Eltham: our public horror at racism has increased.

Case studies...

Meet two friends who live in Eltham, south London, where Stephen Lawrence died. They share the same hopes. But the national figures suggest the prospects for any black person are much less favourable than for someone who is white...

Mimi Olaide, 19, lives in Eltham with his sister, Christana, 22, mother, a mental health nurse, and father, who can't work for health reasons. They rent from a housing association. They moved there in 2010. Mimi is in his second year studying sports science and PE at St Mary's University College in Twickenham.

'I want to be a PE teacher. Whatever grade I get in the third year will determine what I do. I want to go on and do a PGCE [Postgraduate Certificate in Education] or GTP [Graduate Teaching Programme] and you need a minimum of a 2.1. Have I been affected by racism? Not me directly, I don't think so. There's maybe just local gang rivalry, but that's non-racial. Eltham used to be really racist. Obviously I was at uni last week, people were asking how Eltham is, because they know Stephen Lawrence was killed there. There are lots of multicultural people around

ikely to go to jail than their white counterparts when convicted of similar crimes – and they serve longer sentences. A Ministry of Justice (MoJ) analysis of tens of thousands of cases found that in 2010, 23 per cent of white defendants were sent to prison for indictable offences, compared with 27 per cent of black counterparts and 29 per cent of Asian defendants.

The report, *Statistics on Race and the Criminal Justice System*, also found that ethnic minority defendants received longer sentences in almost every offence group. For sexual offences, white defendants received an average of just over four years in jail, but black defendants were sent down for more than five years. For violence against the person, the average breakdown was 16.8 months for whites, 20 months for blacks and almost two years for Asian defendants. The MoJ insisted that 'the identification of differences should not be equated with discrimination', claiming that the disparities between ethnic groups could be explained by the seriousness of the offences, the presence of mitigating or aggravating factors and whether or not a defendant pleaded guilty.

Yet Lee Jasper, chairman of the London Race and Criminal Justice Consortium, said: 'Nothing can so starkly illustrate the industrial scale of racism in the judicial process than these figures.'

Last summer's riots paradoxically suggested something in society has changed for the better. The ingredients for widespread inter-racial violence were there, but it never materialised. However, Gurbux Singh, who was chair of the Commission for Racial Equality when Oldham and Bradford were torn by race riots in 2001, warned yesterday: 'With the recession taking hold, when you have disaffected young people who feel they are right at the bottom competing with another community, I am fearful that the tensions can easily arise again.'

In March 1993, a month before Stephen's murder, Stoke City player Mark Stein was called a 'short, ugly, black, bean-headed twat' by an opponent on the football pitch. On Friday, Tom Adeyemi, the 20-year-old Oldham defender, was left in tears after alleged racist abuse was hurled at him from Liverpool's Kop. A 20 year-old man from Aintree was arrested last night in relation to the incident.

now, compared to how Eltham used to be. It's not as racist now as people say it was then.'

Luke Kimberley, 21, has always lived in Eltham. He lives with his mother, who works in student finance at South Bank University, father, a taxi driver, and sister Elle, 18. He is in his third year studying PE at St Mary's University College in Twickenham

'I want to be a PE teacher. If I want to go into that I'll have to do a PGCE. That's really my main ambition at the moment. Buying a house, that's my main goal, a normal lifestyle really, nothing extravagant. Mum and Dad own a house and I'd like to follow in their footsteps. Mimi plays in the same football team as me at uni. We don't meet up when we come back here, only at uni. Racism is quite a talking point at the moment. I have a range of friends from different ethnic backgrounds. As far as I know they haven't experienced any racism. Probably there is racism in Eltham, but not as much as everyone makes out there is. Obviously the attack on Stephen Lawrence was a racist one, but I don't think Eltham in itself is racist.'

Crime

Crime continues to be one of the most controversial sources of racial tension between the police and local communities. Disproportionate use of stop and search remains widespread – with a massive difference in how different ethnic groups are treated. Black men are 26 times more likely than their white counterparts to be stopped and searched under the Criminal Justice and Public Order Act. Black people also have a higher chance of being arrested and imprisoned than their white counterparts. They even face stiffer sentences for the same crimes – black offenders are 44 per cent more likely to be given a prison sentence for driving offences.

Serious inequalities remain within the police, with the Met having almost no senior ethnic minority officers above the rank of superintendent. The ongoing tensions in communities were highlighted when the shooting by police of a young black man in Tottenham sparked last summer's riots.

Millions of Britons are denied justice by the persistence of racism, Lord Macdonald, former Director of Public Prosecutions, said last Friday. Describing racism as a 'tubercular virus lurking in the shadows' he added: 'We should not deny those millions of people for whom the comfort of social justice is still not constantly there, those people who still live, through no choice of their own, outside its embrace and protection.'

The disproportionate number of black people stopped and searched by the police continues to be a 'national scandal', said Trevor Phillips, chairman of the Equality and Human Rights Commission, last week.

Dr Aisha K Gill

Reader in criminology, University of Roehampton

'There is strong evidence that black people are over-represented throughout the criminal justice process. In the last two decades we have seen a punitive trend in criminal justice policy, and the changes in police practice that accompany it have negative consequences for BME communities. Indeed the growth in the expansion of proactive policing and in police and prosecutorial powers have disproportionately affected BME communities.'

Education

The Prime Minister rattled Oxford University last year when he described its low intake of black students as 'disgraceful'. He was wrong to claim it only accepted one black student in 2009 – it actually took one 'black Caribbean' person out of a total of 27 black students for undergraduate study that year. Nevertheless, everyone seemed to agree with his assertion: 'We have got to do better than that.'

In fact, there is no shortage of ethnic minority undergraduates: nearly one in five in 2010, an increase of almost a third since 1994.

But look at the number of ethnic minorities at 'good' universities and a different picture emerges. According to the Equality and Human Rights Commission, fewer than ten per

cent of black students are at Russell Group universities, compared to a quarter of white students. Head teachers in England's schools are also overwhelmingly white – some 95 per cent in 2010, with less than one per cent from black Caribbean or African backgrounds.

But when it comes to pupils achieving five GCSEs above grade C, progress has been made. The best school performers in 2010 were the Chinese with 90 per cent getting these grades. Asians were next, followed by mixed race pupils. Almost two-thirds of black students got the grades, only one percentage point behind their white contemporaries. But black Caribbean boys continue to lag.

Tony Sewell

Chair of the London inquiry into schools and founder of the charity Generating Genius

'During the 1990s, I used to teach Doreen Lawrence [Stephen's mother] at an adults' college in Woolwich. Then, education was thought to be how you got a better life. The stumbling block now is aspiration. This is not a problem of race, but of class and caste. There has been a long period of anti-racism education but I am not convinced it's had much impact on black children. The fastest improving group is Nigerian girls; two groups standing still are black Caribbean boys and working-class white boys.'

Jobs

In 1993, the British economy was emerging from the end of a recession that hit most of the population, but the ethnic communities were still suffering disproportionate levels of unemployment. A TUC survey in that year estimated that, while the jobless rate had risen to nearly 12 per cent for whites, the figure for black people was twice that number. A period of growth improved employment and narrowed the gap between ethnic groups – although the latest 13.3 per cent unemployment rate among non-whites is still almost double the figure recorded for whites.

A new recession has triggered fresh concerns that any progress ould be reversed: for example, council cutbacks are likely to have a disproportionate impact on the high numbers of black and minority ethnic (BME) workers at local authorities. Activists have complained that groups have been lagging behind in crucial areas of the labour market even during the boom years.

Black people in their early twenties are twice as likely to be not in employment, education or training (Neet) as white people; although 14 per cent of the working-age population in England are from ethnic minorities, only seven per cent of apprenticeships were filled by BME candidates. BME workers, even many graduates, are generally paid less than white counterparts. Rates of self-employment among black workers are significantly lower than the national average.

For some, this is compelling evidence of institutionalised racism in the labour market. But others point to an equally troubling development: self-imposed limits on aspirations.

Jeremy Crook, OBE

Director, Black Training and Enterprise Group

'Things are still pretty bad in the labour market. Young black people in particular have a negative portrayal which damages their chances of getting jobs – and, I think, their own expectations. We were involved in the Reach programme two years ago, which gave young BME people role models, and the feedback we had was that coming into contact with black people in the professions and other areas raised their aspirations.

But it is still hard for them to succeed when they are not getting a fair chance from employers, from training schemes or from banks that are not lending enough to black-run businesses.'

Media

The media are rarely shy to shout out 'racism', and rightly so, but it wasn't until Greg Dyke called the BBC 'hideously white' more than ten years ago that pundits began to look inwards.

In 1996, less than five per cent of staff in Carlton TV newsrooms was

from minority ethnic backgrounds; by 2010, the number of ethnic minorities at ITV was ten per cent – higher than the 7.9 per cent UK average. BBC and Channel 4 have a 12 and 13 per cent minority ethnic workforce respectively, but this drops to six per cent in BBC senior management.

Just over five per cent of adverts in 2010 used actors from a non-white background, while ethnic minorities represent about 13 per cent of the population. In 2002, the Journalism Forum found that 96 per cent of journalists were white. Ethnic minorities are chronically underrepresented in national newspapers. The IoS has a small staff, of whom two come from ethnic minority backgrounds.

Krishnan Guru-Murthy

Channel 4 News presenter

'TV has changed massively in 18 years, in terms of diversity. Portrayal is also much better than when I was a kid, but in many ways things haven't changed. After a couple of decades of very well-intended initiatives, we have failed to deliver people from diverse backgrounds at the top. There are reasonable numbers of middle-class people from Indian origin, like me [in broadcasting], but it's much harder to encourage working-class Bangladeshis, or African Caribbeans, or Chinese. It's straightforward what we need: ways to benchmark success and sanctions when you don't achieve the diversity you want to.'

Parliament

When Diane Abbott provoked a storm on Twitter over her 'white people love playing divide and rule' comment last week, we were reminded that she was the first female black MP in the House of Commons, elected in 1987. At the time of Stephen Lawrence's death in 1993, she was one of just six ethnic minority MPs in Westminster.

This has increased more than four-fold to 28; the most recent addition was Labour's Seema Malhotra when she won Feltham and Heston by-election last month. There are 17 Labour MPs and 11 Conservatives – but not a single ethnic minority candidate has won a seat for the Lib Dems at a general election. Only Parmjit Singh

Gill, who won the Leicester South by-election in 2004 only to lose it at the 2005 election, has represented the third party in the Commons.

In government, the numbers are bleaker: in 2002, Paul Boateng made history by becoming the first black cabinet minister. But progress has stalled. The only ethnic minority person with a seat at the cabinet table is Baroness Warsi, despite David Cameron's promise to make his party more reflective of British society.

David Lammy

Labour MP for Tottenham

'On the face of it, Parliament is changing. But we should not rejoice just yet. We live in a age of dangerous political apathy. The fact that Parliament looks and sounds completely different from the modern Britain it is supposed to represent is a further obstacle. Does British politics feel any more relevant to the black man in Moss Side, the Muslim lady from Sparkbrook or the Turkish family in Dalston today than it did in 1993? Sadly, the answer is no.'

Legal

Despite claims of strenuous attempts at change from within, the upper echelons of the legal profession remain predominantly white. To a degree, the stereotype that judges are white, male, privately educated and from the Home Counties is often not far from the mark. Things are improving, but at a very slow pace. In 1998, 1.6 per cent of the judiciary was not white; now that figure is nearly five per cent.

The first non-white High Court judge, Justice Linda Dobbs, was not appointed until 2004. She had said: 'While this appointment might be seen as casting me into the role of standard bearer, I am simply a practitioner following a career path. I am confident, nevertheless, that I am the first of many to come.' But since then, only one more person from an ethnic minority background has been brought into the senior judiciary.

Among solicitors and barristers the picture is slightly more optimistic. Where once you would have struggled to find a black or Asian face in a wig and gown, now about one in ten barristers are from an ethnic minority.

Courtenay Griffiths

Barrister

'When you go into a court like the Old Bailey on any one day, some 90 per cent of the defendants will be black, and yet you'll find it hard to find a black face prosecuting. I think it's a shame that we have only two non-white judges and not enough women. But one has to realise that it takes 20 to 25 years to grow a judge. The vast majority of black and ethnic minority entrants to the bar have just not spent enough time within the profession to reach this position, so no amount of pushing will achieve that until we have a cadre of black lawyers that reach that level.'

Sport

Black athletes outside football see relatively little racism, but Britain's biggest sporting money-spinner is another matter altogether. Just months after Stephen Lawrence was killed, a campaign to kick racism out of football was launched with some fanfare. At that time, black players were routinely abused or spat upon by 'fans'. The increasing number of black players in the game, along with action by clubs and anti-racist groups, have combined to drive out the public racism that used to characterise football.

But a series of recent incidents, most notably the suspension of Liverpool player Luis Suarez for racist behaviour to Man Utd's Patrice Evra, and the decision to prosecute England captain John Terry for alleged racism towards West Ham's Anton Ferdinand, highlights how racism remains under the surface.

And while black players are a common sight on the pitch, there are hardly any black faces to be seen in club boardrooms – with just two black managers in the entire football league.

Social networking sites are now being used by racist fans. Northumbria Police yesterday began an investigation after ex-Premier League star and football pundit Stan

Collymore was allegedly the victim of racist abuse on Twitter. It is believed the tweets in question were sent by someone in the Tyneside area. A 21-year-old has been arrested in connection with the matter.

Some 18 years after the launch of Let's Kick Racism Out of Football, the issue is put in context by news that Oldham player Tom Adeyemi was reduced to tears this weekend by racist abuse from fans during an FA Cup game away at Liverpool.

Lord Ouseley

Chairman of Kick It Out and former head of the CRE

'Going to watch football in the early 1990s was an unpleasant experience. You had to be very careful. If you weren't with people who would look after you and weren't in parts of the ground where it was safe to go, you just wouldn't go. At that time black footballers active in football, like John Fashanu, would say their families would stop going because the abuse was so extensive – being spat at, booed, all sorts of unbelievable behaviour... There have been huge strides forward since then, and the nastiness and the worst excesses of both abuse and violence have to a large extent gone.'

Entertainment

On the face of it, the entertainment industry appears to be an area where there has been progress in racial equality. From singers such as Rihanna and Dizzee Rascal to award-winning film and TV stars like Dev Patel and Sophie Okonedo, our screens seem less whitewashed than two decades ago. But while more than half of last year's top-20 music artists were not white, most of the people managing them still are.

Some of our most talented actors still feel they need to move abroad to find fulfilling roles. Actors such as Idris Elba – best known for *Luther* and *The Wire* – have decamped to the US after finding the parts he was offered in the UK were too few and too one-dimensional. David Harewood, star of *Blood Diamond* who was made an MBE in the latest honours list, said in a

recent interview that he was 'slight[ly] conflicted' about winning the awar[d]. 'Although it is a great honour, I st[ill] feel there is a hell of a lot of wo[rk] to be done here... Looking at the T[V] schedules over Christmas, I did n[ot] see many black faces in dramas.'

Non-white actors – on stage an[d] in film and TV – still struggle. Ju[st] 0.7 per cent of members of Equi[ty] describe themselves as 'Blac[k] Caribbean', 0.4 per cent as India[n,] 0.1 per cent as Pakistani and non[e] as Bangladeshi.

While a quarter of London[workers are from an ethnic minori[ty] background, only seven per cen[t] of those who work in the capital['s] film industry are. The figure wa[s] three per cent 30 years ago, and th[e] broadcasting union Bectu says it w[ill] take 120 years at the current rate f[or] it to reflect the demographics of th[e] London workforce.

Jazzie B

Founder of Soul II Soul, musi[c] producer and entrepreneur

'In 1987 I only saw one black perso[n] in the music industry on the other [of] the fence. She was called Sandr[a] Scott and worked for Virgin [?] records. We're still friends. No[w] I've met a few black manager[s] and black people working in th[e] background, but I've yet to see on[e] of them sign a cheque. On televisio[n] I actually think it's weird that there['s] no programming on any station tha[t] truly represents us in a positive ligh[t.] Everyone thinks it's all great, but [I] don't know if there are any blac[k] people working in commissioning[.] We should be light years ahead o[f] this now.'

8 January 2012

⇨ The above article original[ly] appeared in *The Independen[t]* and is reprinted with permission[.] Please visit www.independen[t.] co.uk for further information.

Spotlight on racial violence: January – June 2012

An overview of racial violence and harassment in the first six months of 2012.

The Institute of Race Relations (IRR), which documents racist attacks, is now collating regular short briefings on emerging trends in racial violence throughout the UK. And the first six months of 2012 reveals a reality of routine abuse and harassment – from graffiti to vicious assault, from alcohol-fuelled vandalism to hate campaigns. At least one attack has proved fatal. Given that these incidents were recorded in the local or (much less frequently) national press, they show only a tiny fraction of the true scale of violence. (51,187 racist incidents were recorded by the police in 2010/11, the last year for which statistics are available.) Nonetheless, they do provide a snapshot of the reach and impact of popular racism.

Racist abuse is high on the public agenda at the moment. Or, to be more specific, racist abuse which is carried out by footballers or has footballers as the victims is high on the agenda. This is unsurprising. When the England captain has been embroiled in allegations that he racially abused another Premier League player, when high-profile footballers are routinely peppered with racist insults through their Twitter accounts or when players are made to endure racist chants by opposing (or their own, for that matter) 'fans', it has all the ingredients for a media frenzy. It is a fixation which is reflected in countless blogs, documentaries and column inches and, at the very least, it has forced a re-evaluation of the carefully cultivated façade that racism in the sport is now in the past.

Rarefied though footballers' lives may be, what happens on the pitch is actually a good indicator of the way racism percolates the lives of people on a daily basis. Quickly and easily a culture of casual racism, largely unacknowledged, and supposedly consigned to the past, can turn into racist abuse and violence.

Many of the cases which we document below make clear that certain workers remain at high risk of abuse and attack – especially those who ply their trade in the night-time economy as taxi drivers, staff in convenience stores, takeaway workers and employees in off-licences. They also show attacks on the streets taking place in the context of what at first seem minor altercations, but rapidly morph into brutal violence. Like many of the examples of racist abuse that have taken place in relation to football, these are cases which show how the most petty, trivial frustrations can trigger brutal racial violence; where a prejudice just beneath the surface of day-to-day reality can quickly and unexpectedly manifest itself in abuse, threats and assault. Witness the man who threatened to burn a shop down in Crosby a few months ago, calling the Asian workers 'rats' and squirting cleaning fluid into one of their faces simply because he was refused a bottle of vodka on credit; the man who went on a spree of violence in a chip shop in Liverpool, racially abusing Asian staff members and attacking customers simply because he asked for tissues and felt he was given too few; the man in Birmingham who, infuriated at not being able to watch a certain film at a cinema, vented his anger by ripping off a woman's niqab.

Of course, this is not to say that racist attacks do not always take place without any foresight or planning. Disturbingly, our research also exposes a trend of racist attacks against children, families and parents with their children, some of which involve ongoing, organised campaigns of harassment, terrorising families in their own homes. In Kidderminster, for example, a child's pet rabbit was mutilated and hung up in full view in a sadistic incident which made up only one part of a long-standing 'hate' campaign. In Salford, meanwhile, a black woman pushing her baby in a pram was racially abused by a man who went on to throw acid over her which burnt through her clothes and left her needing hospital treatment. And in Edinburgh, a 12-year-old Asian schoolgirl, who had been called a 'P*ki bastard' on Facebook, was attacked by about ten other schoolgirls who took it in turns to kick her in her head, beating her with such force that she was left with double vision.

Taken together, the attacks which we document give a glimpse of a reality of racial violence which occurs day-in-day-out, up and down the UK, from the most rural of villages to large cities. At the same time, our monitoring also indicates that supporters of far-right groups remain prepared to resort to violence and destruction in order to make their presence felt. For all of the English Defence League's (EDL) PR spin about peaceful protest, for example, for all of its vapid manoeuvring, attempting to present itself as an organisation upholding and promoting human rights, the reality is that its marches frequently continue to descend into drunken bullying and violence, supporters continue to attack people, and the Internet remains a medium through which supporters peddle racist abuse.

Below is a selection of those attacks which have taken place between 1 January and 30 June 2012.

Targeting young people, families or mothers with children

June 2012: Officers from Brighton and Hove council were called to investigate a 'culture of racial abuse' at a school in Brighton, where black and 'mixed race' pupils were routinely being bullied, harassed and in some cases physically attacked. One girl had been forced to flee from a gang of pupils attacking her, of whom one threatened her with a knuckleduster. (*Brighton Argus*, 8 July 2012)

28 May 2012: Amara Jaffer, a 13-year-old schoolgirl, was among the victims of a series of racially motivated attacks in Gloucester. Amara was just a few metres from her home when the driver and occupants of a passing Transit van sprayed her in the face with an unknown liquid. Other victims, in separate attacks by the same people, said they were racially abused. (*Gloucester Citizen*, 30 May 2012)

22 May 2012: A 30-year-old Asian woman playing with her three children in a park in Manchester was told by three teenage girls to take her children away from the swings. The teenagers then racially abused and kicked her, before a man with the teenagers indecently exposed himself to the woman. (*Manchester Evening News*, 25 May 2012)

22 March 2012: A black woman who was pushing her baby in a pram in Salford was left with permanent scars after a white man racially and sexually abused her before throwing acid in her face. (*Voice*, 26 March 2012)

13 February 2012: A woman from Thailand travelling on a bus in Plymouth with her four-year-old child was subjected to a torrent of racist abuse by five teenagers who spat on her, mocked her accent and carried on abusing her when, sobbing, she approached the bus-driver for help. (*Plymouth Herald*, 19 March 2012)

Attacks, graffiti and threats by supporters of far-right groups

28 June 2012: A swastika was spray-painted on a front door in Fleetwood, as well as obscenities written on a window and a car damaged. (*Fleetwood Weekly*, 19 July)

19 June 2012: A community centre in Blackburn was daubed with graffiti, including numerous racist insults and a swastika. (*Lancashire Telegraph*, 21 June 2012)

22 May 2012: The Haamara Centre in Preston was broken into by vandals who caused extensive internal damage. Windows were smashed and the walls were covered in racist graffiti as well as swastikas. (*Lancashire Evening Post*, 28 May 2012)

2 March 2012: An EDL supporter told an Asian taxi-driver that he was 'not welcome here', pointing to EDL slogans on his T-shirt and launching a tirade of abuse. When he was arrested he sang EDL songs and police later found anti-Muslim posts on his Facebook page. (*Daventry Express*, 6 March 2012)

Anti-Muslim attacks not known to involve far-right groups

June 2012: Several graves in the Muslim section of a cemetery in Leeds, including the grave of one of the perpetrators of the July 2005 terrorist attacks in London, were vandalised. Headstones were pulled over and offensive messages were scrawled on them. (*BBC News*, 15 June 2012)

2 April 2012: Firefighters were called to a mosque in Luton after two bins were pushed against one of its doors and set alight. A representative of the mosque said Muslim leaders suspected that the attack was deliberate. (*Luton Herald & Post*, 2 April 2012)

Workers at risk of attack

4 June 2012: A man was arrested after staff at a newsagent in Liverpool claimed he subjected them to racist abuse. A month earlier, Sam Harrison, 19, was jailed for manslaughter for stabbing Mahesh Wickramasingha, a man who worked at the same newsagent. Some of the staff members who were abused had been present when the stabbing had taken place, and the owner of the business said that he had had to cancel a vigil in the shop in memory of Mahesh due to safety fears. (*Liverpool Echo*, 1 June 2012)

19 May 2012: Harun Shah Zaman, a taxi driver in Leicester, was brutally beaten and robbed by four passengers. One of the passengers headbutted him and another punched him in the face before the other two (female) passengers joined in the assault. The group then stole his wallet, his cash bag, his keys and his sat nav (which they smashed on the floor) and ran off. Despite there being several witnesses to the attack, nobody intervened. (*Leicester Mercury*, 21 May 2012)

Street attacks

June 2012: A Polish man talking on his mobile phone was approached by three white males who began racially abusing him. One of the men then punched him in the face, fracturing his cheek bone, before the trio ran away. (*Runcorn and Widnes World*, 22 June 2012)

6 May 2012: A group of Slovakian men were sitting on a beach in Hastings, waiting for a friend, when several men began kicking gravel at them and making racist comments. Although the Slovakian men walked away, the attackers followed them and assaulted them before running away. (*Hastings Observer*, 4 June 2012)

Racism in football

4 June 2012: About 150 England fans in Bedford targeted Italian supporters after Italy knocked England out of the 2012 European Championship. The Italian fans had formed a cavalcade of vehicles to celebrate and some of the cars were damaged, as well as one Italian fan attacked. (BBC News, 25 June 2012)

15 April 2012: Chelsea fan Stephen Fitzwater was banned from football matches for three years after he was heard racially abusing Chelsea striker Didier Drogba in an FA Cup semi-final game against Tottenham. (*Metro*, 3 May 2012)

26 January 2012: Queens Park Rangers defender Anton Ferdinand was sent death threats through the post, along with a shotgun cartridge, ahead of a game against Chelsea. John Terry, Chelsea's captain, had been charged by the police of committing a racially aggravated offence against Anton Ferdinand in 2011 (a charge which in July 2012 he was acquitted of). (*Daily Mirror*, 27 January 2012)

1 January 2012: A 16-year-old student was ordered to carry out 100 hours of community service after racially abusing Inverness Caledonian Thistle striker Gregory Tade and telling him to 'give up life' on Twitter. (BBC News, 18 May 2012)

26 July 2012

⇨ The above information is reprinted with kind permission from the Institute of Race Relations. Please visit www.irr. org.uk for further information.

Islamophobia filtering into classrooms

A recent BBC report looking into racism in schools found nearly 88,000 racist incidents took place in UK schools over a four-year period. However, the Coalition Government have removed the duty of schools to report all racist incidents. The report also showed a rise in Islamophobia in the classroom.

In 2007 the then Labour Government said schools in England and Wales must monitor and report all racist incidents following the enquiry into the murder of Stephen Lawrence. But the present Conservative-led Government have removed this rule and subsequently fewer incident have been reported.

In a BBC article Sarah Soyei from Show Racism the Red Card (SRRC), said:

'We are seeing a real increase in racism in some areas which is down to factors like a growth of Islamophobia in society which is filtering into classrooms.'

What's more, in many cases teachers would not be told of a racist incident due to the victim feeling intimidated and the fear of repercussions, as well as teachers not recognising racist bullying. Ms Soyei adds in the article:

'Racism is a very real issue in many classrooms around the country, but cases of racist bullying are notoriously underreported.

The recently launched Tell Mama (measuring anti-Muslim attacks) project, was set up to record reported crimes specific to the Muslim community enabling the project to support the victims of anti-Muslim incidents and hate crimes.

Fiyaz Mughal (OBE) from Tell Mama commenting on the report said:

'This report by the BBC confirms what we are picking up in the Tell Mama project that school environments are places where hate incidents can and do take place. Whilst the project has just been launched, we are picking up cases where Muslim women have been abused because they are identifiable as Muslims, either because they wear the Hijab or the Niqab and some of them fear going to schools to drop their children off. This is a situation where no parent should find themselves within.'

But unions and anti-racism charities believe the Government's relaxed approach to the reporting of racist bullying is a big mistake.

Christine Blower, general secretary of the National Union of Teachers, said:

'It is not just a box-ticking exercise, we absolutely do need recording and reporting of all racist incidents,'

The Department of Education believe it is teachers and parents who need to deal with racism in schools. But without recorded incidents it is quite easy to overlook the problem and subsequently make racist attacks easier to get away with.

14 June 2012

⇨ Information from Awaaz. Please visit www.awaaznews.com for further information.

Racism in the classroom

Information from About Equal Opportunities.

Racism is the unfair treatment of, or outright hatred of, individuals of a certain race. Sometimes racism or racial discrimination is described at the organisational level, as a system or policy of treating one (or multiple) races unfairly. Racism may be practised to benefit one race, or simply because one or more other races are thought to be inferior. Unfortunately, racism may still exist in classrooms across the United Kingdom.

Racism and the law

The Race Relations Act 1976 and all of its amendments and extensions protect individuals from being discriminated against on the grounds of colour, race, nationality, religious beliefs or ethnicity. This Act does not distinguish between whether racist practices were done on purpose or not, it is concerned only with the fact that racial discrimination occurred. This Act covers discrimination faced in employment, education and more.

Racism and education

Racism can be experienced in four main ways. Direct discrimination is deliberate and obvious. Indirect discrimination occurs when practices or policies disadvantage one or more racial groups. Harassment occurs when an environment is allowed to become hostile for members of a certain race. Finally, victimisation occurs when someone has complained about racism and is then treated less fairly than others. These actions are all in breach of the Race Relations Act 1976 and its amendments and extensions. In terms of education, racism can be experienced by a pupil of an institution as well as by an individual seeking entrance to a certain institution.

Racist bullying by other pupils

Racist bullying by other pupils can take many forms, from hurtful comments to physical attacks. In order to stop such bullying, students should first familiarise themselves with their school's anti-bullying policy. Then students should record instances of bullying in a diary, including what happened and who was involved, and tell a trusted adult about the incidents. Any proof of bullying, such as defaced property or hurtful electronic communications, should be saved. Online abuse, whether via text messages, emails, instant messages, websites or blogs, should also be saved. When ready, the student and his or her parents should confront the school and make a formal complaint according to the school's procedures and policies.

Racist bullying by teachers

Though despicable, bullying by teachers may occur. Teachers may make degrading comments about a student, engage in unwanted or hostile physical contact with a student, make unwanted or suggestive sexual contact with a student, say inappropriate or lewd things to or about a student, or even suggest to a student that his or her grade depends on something other than his or her studies. If a student feels that they are being subjected to racist bullying or discrimination by a teacher, the student should ask for a meeting with both the teacher and the department head. Parents may want to be at this meeting as well. If it is believed that nothing has come from the meeting then a formal complaint should be filed with the school. In the meantime, the student should discuss transfer options as a way of being removed from that teacher's class. It may not be fair that the student has to leave, but safety should be the first priority.

Racism is disgusting in all forms, but unfortunately it does still exist. Individuals who encounter racism in the classroom should be prepared to document and report this type of bullying. If the educational institution itself does not respond to these complaints then it might be wise to seek professional, legal advice about the situation.

15 September 2012

⇨ The above information is reprinted with kind permission from About Equal Opportunities. Please visit www.aboutequalopportunities. co.uk for further information.

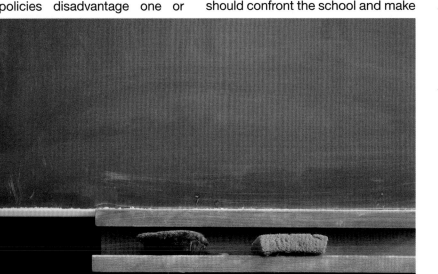

Integration in England today

An extract from the Communities and Local Government report *Creating the conditions for integration.*

Our history and our shared values mean we are better placed than many other countries to meet the challenges of integration.

First, there is a long history of migration both to and from these shores. Over the course of centuries people from different countries have settled here, learnt English, acquired new skills, and worked hard to provide for their families. They have enriched their neighbourhoods and the country as a whole, and made major contributions to national and local life.

England's second major advantage is a tradition of tolerance. The overwhelming majority of us believe in treating people fairly and with respect, no matter what their background. It is one of our strongest, and proudest, shared values and one which we must continually protect. This belief in treating all people fairly underpins the Government's commitment to equality for all, and this paper on integration is complementary to the wider Government commitments to equalities and social mobility, including the Equality Act 2010, Equality Strategy, and Social Mobility Strategy.

The result is that today, across the country, people from different backgrounds get on well together. Most people feel they belong to their neighbourhood and to this country, and have a sense of pride in the place where they live. Immigration has often brought benefits to both settled communities and newcomers and produced some of England's most successful figures in business, sports, arts, politics and philanthropy.

The last decade has brought fresh challenges, however. We have seen an increase in international travel and the expansion of the European Union, with substantial and sustained increases in migration into the UK from both within and outside the EU. The resulting pace of change in our local communities is unprecedented. Most places have accommodated the changes, but there is no room for complacency. Since 2001, concern about race relations, immigrants or immigration has been an important issue with latest data (from December 2011) showing that with around one in five (22 per cent) of people say it is an important issue.

A small number of places have experienced problems, with established communities unable to respond to the pace of change, and incoming migrants to some communities unable or unwilling to integrate. The Prime Minister has talked about ensuring greater control over immigration to make it a source of national strength rather than a concern.

There are also other challenges facing us at this point. The disturbances that occurred in a number of English towns and cities in August 2011 highlighted some deep-seated challenges we need to tackle. But it is important not to oversimplify these serious events. These were not race riots. The perpetrators and victims of the disturbances were from a wide range of backgrounds, as were the local residents who came together afterwards to clean up their streets. The challenge is how to respond to the criminality and lack of social responsibility that lay behind the actions of a small number of people.

We must understand and protect the values, experiences and opportunities which bring people together to act on issues which matter to them.

We believe that core values and experience must be held in common. We should be robustly promoting British values such as democracy, rule of law, equality of opportunity and treatment, freedom of speech and the rights of all men and women to live free from persecution of any kind. It is these values which make it possible for people to live and work together, to bridge boundaries between communities and to play a full role in society. When this is underpinned both by opportunities to succeed, and a strong sense of personal and social responsibility to the society which has made success possible, the result is a strong society. There are therefore five key factors which we believe contribute to integration:

Common ground

A clear sense of shared aspirations and values, which focuses on what we have in common rather than our differences.

Responsibility

A strong sense of our mutual commitments and obligations, which brings personal and social responsibility.

Social mobility

People able to realise their potential to get on in life.

Participation and empowerment

People of all backgrounds have the opportunities to take part, be heard and take decisions in local and national life.

Tackling intolerance and extremism

A robust response to threats, whether discrimination, extremism or disorder, that deepen division and increase tensions.

7 February 2012

⇨ The above information is reprinted with kind permission from Communities and Local Government. Please visit www.communities.gov.uk.

White people paid more and ethnic pay gap widening

Researchers from the University of Essex found that in 1993 white people earned an average of 18p an hour more than non-whites, but by 2008 the gap had risen to 43p an hour. This was around 7.5% of the minimum wage for those over 21 in 2008 or 3.6% of median hourly earnings.

The research by Dr Malcolm Brynin at ISER and Dr Ayse Güveli, from the Department of Sociology at the University of Essex found that Britian's white workers are paid more than ethnic minorities and the hourly pay gap has more than doubled in the 15 years to 2008.

The research published in the latest edition of the journal *Work, employment and society*, Dr Brynin and Dr Güvel analysed more than 650,000 results from UK's large-scale quarterly Labour Force Survey.

'The gap between whites and non-whites was caused because non-whites found it harder to get into well-paid professions and trades'

They say that most of the gap between whites and non-whites was caused because non-whites found it harder to get into well-paid professions and trades.

The analysis shows not only that the ethnic pay gap varies considerably by ethnic minority but that it is in large measure the result of occupational segregation.

However, even where the two groups worked in the same profession or trade, there was a gap in pay – by 2008 whites were earning an average of 43p an hour more than non-whites doing the same type of work. This compared to 1993 when whites earned an average of 18p an hour more than non-whites in the same profession or trade.

'In Britain white people earn more than people from ethnic minorities on average'

They found that the overall gap had widened despite the fact that the proportion of people in most ethnic minorities groups working in managerial jobs was about the same as whites by 2008 – around 45%. This was probably because non-whites tended to be in lower levels in the job hierarchy.

'In Britain white people earn more than people from ethnic minorities on average. However, this gap is generally less when the pay of white people is compared to that of ethnic minorities within occupations. The wage gap therefore derives in significant measure from occupational segregation. Where a negative pay gap occurs it is because ethnic minorities tend to cluster into low-paying occupations.'

'This sorting is due in part to personal factors such as education but some is almost undoubtedly because minorities find it harder to enter better paid occupations.'

'When we try to understand the determinants of wages controlling for a range of factors, it is clear that on this basis most ethnic minorities earn consistently less than white people, if not always by much. One implication is that some minorities do not earn as much as their education would warrant.'

28 August 2012

⇨ The above information is reprinted with kind permission from the Institute for Social & Economic Research. Please visit www.iser.essex.ac.uk for further information.

Welcome to the interview Mr... John Smith?

It used to be Mohammed Ahmed, but for some reason I just wasn't getting any interviews...

Race to the top: the experiences of black students in higher education

A target paper produced by the Elevation Networks Trust and published by its partner, The Bow Group.

A major report launched today in Parliament by youth employment charity, Elevation Networks, and published by centre-right think tank, the Bow Group, finds that black undergraduates believe there is deep-rooted institutional racism in both politics and major professions. This perception has contributed to lower employment outcomes among recent black graduates than their white counterparts.

With a foreword by Simon Hughes MP, *Race to the Top: The Experiences of Black Students in Higher Education*, the first in a series of reports, produced by Elevation Networks, looks at the experiences of particular groups from non-traditional backgrounds within higher education and the challenges faced by those groups in gaining employment. This first report focuses on the experiences of black students from African and Caribbean backgrounds and is the result of a nationwide consultation, conducted over a two-year period and engaging over 2,500 students. The report was funded by professional services firm Deloitte LLP.

⇨ Black graduates are three times more likely to be unemployed than white graduates within six months of graduation and, should they find employment, they can expect to earn up to 9% less for the same work as a white graduate over five years. Building on these disturbing statistics, the report finds:

⇨ Just under half (47 per cent) of black undergraduates believe Government departments discriminate against black students in their employment policies.

⇨ Black students also feel they would face considerable discrimination when attempting to pursue a career in the legal services, media, fashion and financial services industries.

⇨ 60% of black students do not expect to be in work within six months of graduating and 68% expect to be earning less than £25,000 p.a. in that first graduate role.

⇨ Black students generally believe there is currently not enough mentoring or assistance given in choosing where to go to university and where to find employment.

⇨ Black students generally believe that their parents do not currently receive sufficient guidance from careers counsellors (especially in state schools) to understand the choices available to their children.

⇨ There is a vast discrepancy between the expectations of black students and the outcomes they face following graduation.

Recommendations:

The UK Government should develop a coherent policy framework to tackle race inequality in graduate employment outcomes among students from ethnic minority backgrounds.

The Government should ensure that this policy is sufficiently promoted to change the attitudes of black undergraduates to certain types of employers (especially employers in Government, the legal services, media, fashion and financial services industries).

In publishing league tables at state-funded universities, by way of transparency, the Government should make public figures to illustrate the ethnic background of students currently studying at those universities.

Elevation Networks proposes that, in addition, official higher education data should include an analysis of the academic and employment outcomes of students within institutions, broken down into different ethnic and gender categories.

Elevation Networks calls on the Government to support the expansion of corporate funded diversity mentoring schemes, a version of which Elevation Networks has already piloted through organisations including financial services firms Deloitte LLP, Ernst & Young and HSBC.

State schools should increase the involvement of external careers advisors and funding should be allocated accordingly.

Samuel Kasumu, founder of Elevation Networks, said:

'We hope that the Government takes our findings very seriously. We found that black students were concerned about what their future would be like once they graduated, and many of them believed that the odds were firmly stacked against them. There are particular challenges when it comes to those students who would like to be involved in Government and politics which is very concerning. With the increase in tuition fees, there has never been a more important time to ensure all graduates have an equal chance in the employment market.

Having set up the charity whilst at university, it is a shame to still be talking about the same issues many years later. There are simple actions, like mentoring, that can go a long way in changing the outcomes for many black graduates. But employers and Government must accept that race inequalities must be dealt with collaboratively, with them each playing an active role.'

Richard Mabey, Research Secretary of the Bow Group, said:

'It is a shocking statistic that half of black 16-25-year-olds are unemployed. But, as this research shows, this phenomenon extends also to graduate employment, with black students being three times as likely to be unemployed than white students within six months of graduating.'

Simon Hughes MP said:

'It is clear that many of our institutions of higher education, many leading professional bodies and employers, and Government and Parliament, are all still failing to deliver equal opportunities to young people from all backgrounds.

'Though there is evidence of improvement, there are still too few black youngsters who apply to university, and particularly to the highest ranking universities – which has a harmful knock-on effect on career opportunities after further and higher education.'

'It is certainly the perception of black undergraduates that discrimination is occurring in most of the major graduate professions, including, most strikingly, the civil service. Alongside enterprise and the third sector, Government has a role to play in changing attitudes and creating the necessary conditions for all students to achieve their potential, irrespective of race.'

April 2012

⇨ Information from Elevation Networks. Please visit www.elevationnetworks.org .

A test for racial discrimination, findings

Recruitment practice in British cities.

We applied for nearly a thousand advertised jobs using equivalent job applications. These fictitious applications were randomly assigned names associated with white and minority ethnic groups.

The outcomes of these applications allowed us to estimate the extent of racial discrimination in the early stages of recruitment in British cities. We uncovered significant and widespread discrimination.

⇨ For each job interview invitation, 16 job applications had to be sent from ethnic minority candidates, compared to nine from white candidates.

⇨ Same level of discrimination across all cities and occupations.

⇨ No discrimination found among employers using their own application forms.

⇨ Public sector employers are less likely to discriminate.

⇨ All minority ethnic groups were discriminated against.

For each job interview invitation, 16 job applications had to be sent from ethnic minority candidates, compared to nine from white candidates

The test uncovered a considerable amount of discrimination. We had to send 74 per cent more applications from ethnic minority applicants to get the same level of success. This was despite the applications being equivalent. The only systematic difference between the applications was the name of the applicant.

Same level of discrimination across all cities and occupations

There was little to suggest that discrimination was limited to particular areas or occupations. Although the numbers in our sample were smal there was evidence of similar level of discrimination in all the citie and it was present across all th occupations included in our study.

No discrimination found among employers using their own application forms

We found a very large differenc in discrimination between differer types of applications. There wa essentially no net discriminatio where the process of applyin for the job required the use of th employer's own form. This compare to a high level of discrimination wher application was via a CV.

This may well reflect the fact tha employer forms are often designed s that the section containing persona details (including name) can b detached before the sifting process.

Public sector employers are less likely to discriminate

Public sector employers in our tes were considerably less likely to hav discriminated on the grounds of rac than those in the private sector. Thi may relate to the point above – mor of the public sector organisation in our test required that we use thei form to apply.

All minority ethnic groups were discriminated against

Discrimination appeared to be widespread to the detriment of a minority ethnic groups.

Differences between the minorit ethnic groups included in the stud (black African, black Caribbean Chinese, Indian, Pakistan Bangladeshi) were not significant.

May 2010

⇨ Information from NatCen. www natcen.ac.uk.

Racism and discrimination against gypsies and travellers

Information from Friends Families and Travellers.

Although race relations legislation has been in force in the United Kingdom since 1965 and has developed considerably to protect against increasingly subtle forms of discrimination, gypsies and travellers are still experiencing discrimination of the most overt kind: No blacks, no Irish, no dogs' signs disappeared decades ago, but the 'No travellers' signs, used intentionally to exclude gypsies and travellers, are still widespread, indicating that discrimination against these groups remains the last respectable form of racism in the United Kingdom.

In 2004, Trevor Phillips, the former Chair of the Commission for Racial Equality (CRE), now the Chair of the Equality and Human Rights Commission (EHRC), compared the situation of gypsies and travellers living in Great Britain to that of black people living in the American Deep South in the 1950s and, in 2005, Sarah Spencer, one of the CRE Commissioners, drew further attention to their plight in an article entitled *Gypsies and Travellers: Britain's forgotten minority*:

The European Convention on Human Rights was a key pillar of Europe's response to the Nazi holocaust in which half a million gypsies were among those who lost their lives. The Convention is now helping to protect the rights of this community in the United Kingdom.

The majority of the 15,000 caravans that are homes to gypsy and traveller families in England are on sites provided by local authorities, or which are privately owned with planning permission for this use. But the location and condition of these sites would not be tolerated for any other section of society. 26 per cent are situated next to, or under, motorways, 13 per cent next to runways. 12 per cent are next to rubbish tips, and four per cent adjacent to sewage farms. Tucked away out of sight, far from shops and schools, they can frequently lack public transport to reach jobs and essential services.

In 1997, 90 per cent of planning applications from gypsies and travellers were rejected, compared to a success rate of 80 per cent for all other applications. 18 per cent of gypsies and travellers were homeless in 2003 compared to 0.6 per cent of the general population. Lacking sites on which to live, some pitch on land belonging to others; or on their own land but lacking permission for caravan use. There follows a cycle of confrontation and eviction, reluctant travel to a new area, new encampment, confrontation and eviction. Children cannot settle in school. Employment and health care are disrupted.

Overt discrimination remains a common experience. There is a constant struggle to secure the bare necessities, exacerbated by the inability of many adults to read and write, by the reluctance of local officials to visit sites, and by the isolation of these communities from the support of local residents. But we know that these are communities experiencing severe disadvantage. Infant mortality is twice the national average and life expectancy at least ten years less than that of others in their generation.

Race Relations Act

English gypsies and Irish travellers

Today, both English gypsies and Irish travellers are recognised as distinct ethnic minority groups in law because they are recognised as members of a community with a share history stretching back over hundreds of years. As such they are granted the full protection of the Race Relations Act.

New travellers

New travellers are not a legally recognised ethnic minority group because their history only goes back to the early 1960s. However, all individuals and groups are granted protection under the Human Rights Act.

Types of discrimination

The traveller community faces harassment and discrimination on a daily basis as a result of negative stereotypes and deeply ingrained cultural prejudice. Unfortunately, many instances of harassment and discrimination go unchallenged because they are subtle and indirect. However, there are ways to counter harassment and discrimination and there are specific instances when it can be successfully challenged.

Direct discrimination

Direct discrimination happens when an individual or body (such as a brewery, shop or a service provider, etc.) openly discriminates against an individual or group because of who they are. Examples of this would be things like a pub or shop putting a sign on the door saying 'No Travellers'.

Indirect discrimination

Indirect discrimination happens when a service provider such as a local authority, health authority, school, etc. excludes an individual or group or restricts their access to services because of who they are. Examples of this would be a local authority housing department refusing to put a traveller on a housing waiting list because they have not been resident in the housing authority's area for more than six months. Because travellers face continuous eviction and are often forcibly moved from one area to the next, it is often impossible for them to be resident in one specific locality for a sufficient length of time. The traveller concerned would have to show that they had remained in the general area (i.e. the county and had local links (such a children attending local school or a history of employment).

April 2010

⇨ The above information is reprinted with kind permission from Friends Families and Travellers. Please visit www.gypsy-traveller.org for further information.

Caught in the headlines

Scottish media coverage of Scottish gypsy travellers.

Amnesty International is concerned at the wealth of evidence showing discrimination against Scottish gypsy travellers and the hostility and divisions between Scottish gypsy travellers and settled communities. We believe that both groups lose out from the current situation.

Given the low level of meaningful engagement between the two communities, the media has an important role to play in how settled communities gather information and form opinions about Scottish gypsy travellers. Yet anyone taking a cursory interest in the issue will quickly become aware of mainly hostile press coverage. To get an overview of the situation, we commissioned a media clippings agency to identify all Scottish coverage relating to Scottish gypsy travellers over a four-month period. We received 190 articles which we characterised according to whether each was considered positive, negative or neutral. We also noted the length of each article.

Through that analysis we found:

⇨ With 190 articles in Scotland over four months (or 120 days) there is an average of nearly 1.5 articles a day about Scottish gypsy travellers. Given that there is a very small population of Scottish gypsy travellers (c. 20,000 people, or less than 0.5 per cent of the Scottish population), this group receives a disproportionate level of scrutiny.

⇨ Nearly half (48 per cent) of stories were categorised as presenting an overtly negative picture of Scottish gypsy travellers (with 28 per cent positive and 25 per cent neutral).

⇨ The overwhelming majority of this coverage takes place without the involvement of Scottish gypsy travellers themselves. Only six per cent of the articles presented a community voice so that in the vast majority of cases Scottish gypsy travellers were not afforded any right of reply.

⇨ Certain stereotypes regarding Scottish gypsy travellers featured strongly in the coverage. In particular 38 per cent of the articles made some connection to criminality while 32 per cent brought in reference to dirt and hygiene.

⇨ While local politicians were frequently called upon to comment on Scottish gypsy traveller stories, out of 78 occasions where this occurred only four were characterised as being positive, and 48 as negative

On the basis of this evidence we present the following recommendations:

1) Journalists and editors should adhere to ethical codes of conduct and ethical standards when writing about Scottish gypsy travellers.

2) Journalists should build relationships with Scottish gypsy travellers to ensure balanced reporting.

3) The Scottish Government should take the lead in promoting reconciliation between the settled and Scottish gypsy traveller communities. Political parties should act in a respectful and balanced way when dealing with issues involving Scottish gypsy travellers.

January 2012

⇨ The above information is reprinted with kind permission from Amnesty International. Please visit www.amnesty.org.uk for further information.

Time to hold the media to account for Islamophobia

Information from **The Huffington Post.**

By Dr Nafeez Mosaddeq Ahmed

Over a decade after the terrorist attacks on New York and Washington – and seven years after the London bombings – questions about Islam, Muslims and their place in the wider Western world continue to foment strong debate. One only needs to look at Mehdi Hasan's recent observations on the daily racist vilification he receives as one of only two Muslim columnists in the national media.

So just how much of a problem is anti-Muslim reporting in the British media – and what is its social impact? I set out to answer this question in my new report, *Race and Reform: Islam and Muslims in the British Media*, submitted to the Leveson Inquiry last week.

The report, commissioned and published by Unitas Communications Ltd. – a cross-cultural communications consultancy specialising in Islam–West relations – draws on interviews with a range of media professionals across print and broadcast media in the UK, including journalists and editors from the *Daily Mail*, the *Mail on Sunday*, *Daily Star*, *The Telegraph*, *The Independent on Sunday*, *The Guardian*, *The Times*, Channel 4/ITN and BBC World TV.

My aim was to find out exactly what the existing research to date says about this problem, and how it has tangibly affected the lives of British people – and our conclusions were deeply worrying.

Specialist studies of media coverage on Islam and Muslims over the last two decades demonstrate an overwhelming trend of negative, stereotypical and inaccurate reporting. As Jason Beattie, political editor of the *Daily Mirror,* told us: 'In general, though not exclusively, the portrayal of Muslims in the mainstream media has been unsatisfactory... [including] sloppy and sometimes stereotypical reporting.'

But this isn't because all media outlets sing from the same 'Islamophobic' hymn sheet – far from it. Rather, poor journalistic standards in the populist tabloid press generate inaccurate reporting which tends to set the wider news agenda in print and broadcasting by framing the 'big stories' of the day.

This was the case both before and after 9/11. One study of British broadsheets in the late 1990s, for example, found that they consistently associated the Muslim world with 'extremism and terrorism', 'despotism' and 'sexism'; while reporting of British Muslims focused primarily on 'Muslim violence in the public sphere', including terrorism, faith schools and crime.

Another study of two liberal and conservative British broadsheets between 1994 and 1996 found that 88% of articles on Islam reported the faith as a foreign phenomenon; and that British Muslims were most commonly linked with 'fundamentalism'.

After 9/11, and 7/7, this trend accelerated. A study commissioned by the Greater London Authority of 352 articles over a randomly selected one week period in 2007, found that 91% of articles about Muslims were 'negative'. A wider Channel 4-commissioned survey of 974 British press articles from 2000 to 2008 found two thirds of them to portray British Muslims as a 'threat' and a 'problem', with references to 'radical Muslims' outnumbering references to 'moderates' by 17 to one.

A further big-picture University of Ottawa study of British press representations over the last 15 years found that the biggest shift in reporting after 9/11 was to associate British Muslims with terrorism and extremism; and to associate acts of terrorism with Islamic belief. In all articles on terrorism, the study concluded, the 'Muslimness' of perpetrators of terrorism is emphasised.

So there is no question about it. Reporting on Islam and Muslims in the British media has been predominantly inaccurate, false and racist.

But there is another side to this picture which is, perhaps, even more disturbing. Correlated with the rise in negative media reporting on Muslims, my survey of opinion poll data over the last decade illustrates a rising trend of anti-Muslim sentiment in wider British society. Professor Julian Petley of the Campaign for Press & Broadcasting Freedom points out that, 'if non-Muslims are led to believe that Muslims and Islam pose an existential threat to the "English way of life", then this cannot but seriously damage community cohesion.' Thus, from 2001 to 2006, the number of UK non-Muslims who said they felt threatened by Islam rose from 32% to 53%. By 2010, a further survey found that 75% of non-Muslims now believe Islam is negative for Britain, and that Muslims do not engage positively in society; with 63% not disagreeing that 'Muslims are terrorists.'

This has had a double-whammy impact. On the one hand, media discrimination has contributed to the alienation of some British Muslims. In 2007, 63% of British Muslims felt that UK media portrayals of Muslims were 'Islamophobic' – and 72% of those reported that they 'don't feel a sense of belonging' to Britain.

As Julian Bond, Director of the Christian Muslim Forum, explains, 'even the most engaged, integrated and inter-faith Muslims' finds such negative media portrayals to be 'wearying, frustrating and irritating'.

On the other hand, anti-Muslim hate crimes have risen steadily over the last decade, and are now at record levels. Since 1999, racist offences in general have increased by fourfold – but Muslims are overrepresented as victims in these crimes. The latest Crown Prosecution Service (CPS) figures record a rise of 45% in the number of cases referred to the CPS by police on grounds of religious hostility, and that over most of this decade Muslims accounted for more than 54% of religiously aggravated offences, and are the largest faith group experiencing hate crimes. As of 2010, though only 3% of the population, Muslims represent a massive 44% of those who have died in lethal racist attacks since the 1990s. And police data from two regions over the period 2009 to 2011 documents a total of 1,200 recorded anti-Muslim hate crimes.

And so we come full circle: the predominantly negative and racist reporting on Muslims in the media has promoted an increasingly dangerous anti-Muslim mindset in British society, which in turn has led to an escalation of violent attacks on British Muslims. As former *Daily Star* reporter Richard Peppiatt observes, 'False and inaccurate stories about Muslims routinely put out by the press are, in turn, routinely used as tools by far right groups to legitimise their case

and gain followers. The Interne is full of forums using mainstrear newspaper reporting as proof tha their hateful views about Muslim are true. Unfortunately, newspaper refuse to recognise their role in that

In this context, doing nothing is no an option – to secure a peacefu and cohesive British society fo our children, it is imperative tha the media be held to account fo racist reporting that feeds int the machinations of far-righ criminals. Based on input fron the media professionals anc community leaders we consulted my report thus makes eight ke recommendations to the Levesor Inquiry, among which included more robust enforcemen powers for the Press Complaint: Commission (PCC) to deal wit third-party complaints, with a more equal right of reply anc harsher penalties for violation: of the press code of conduc including fines; a better press cod of conduct revised with assistance from the Equality & Human Right: Commission to ensure medi compliance with existing equalities legislation; establishment of a PCC advisory panel on issues relating to Muslims and minorities; greate engagement between media agencies and minority groups including measures to improve diversity in employment; protectior for journalists from editoria pressure to generate inaccurate stories.

We are not demanding any form of censorship. What we are demanding is very simply tha journalists be tasked to report rea news – not fake it. Is that much to ask?

18 July 2012

⇨ The above information is from *The Huffington Post* and is reprinted with permission from AOL (UK). Please visit www huffingtonpost.co.uk for furthe information.

Prioritise the right battle first: not Islamophobia, but racism

Information from 1st Ethical.

By Abu Eesa Niamatullah

The title isn't exactly brilliant I know because it immediately suggests that one battle is done at the expense of the other. I don't mean that at all of course we should be doing everything we can against all forms of xenophobia and discrimination, but certainly we do need to reassess our priorities as well as perhaps temper slightly our obsession with all things being Islamophobic.

'The Muslim community has been struggling against racism and Islamophobia for a while now'

Racism is always in the headlines, everywhere you are in the world and not just Western or non-Muslim countries. But we obviously concentrate on those areas where we have the biggest chance of bringing about change, and of course that would be the countries which we are citizens of. The last few months have seen the issue of racism ratchet up with the charge against former England football captain John Terry capturing all the front and back pages of the media, a story given new significance when he was cleared of criminal charges but then charged a few days ago by the Football Association, and the plot thickens further with today's announcement that another former England captain, Rio Ferdinand, will also be charged for comments deemed to be racist in nature. And today we had another shocker as a Swiss footballer was sent home from the Olympics in disgrace for a racist tweet. And don't forget the horrific scenes of racism particularly from Eastern European crowds against others running up to and indeed at the European Football Championships in Poland and Ukraine. All this of course is European focused – if we started to extend this to the USA and indeed other countries around the world, this comment-piece would be hijacked.

And even though there are hundreds of such examples happening regularly, the latest racist outrage occurred in a *Daily Mail* editorially approved story as a comment on the Opening Ceremony of the London Olympics. There isn't a single sensible person in this country who doesn't know that the *Daily Mail* is incredibly racist, xenophobic and just an outright hate-mongering unit, but something truly needs to be done against this rising infection of our society.

What is to be done, and how it's to be done is not clear. The Muslim community has been struggling against racism and Islamophobia for a while now, and even the approaches to the problem differ. The majority would quite rightly wish to tackle it head on using the full force of the law, however I am most sympathetic to other views such as that held by the respected commentator Muhammad Amin as expressed recently – in summary his point is that one should focus on fighting for our generic rights as citizens as opposed to making it specific about our religion per se.

I would perhaps say myself that by focusing on racism as our priority, we might be able to cover both bases in one swoop. Have no doubt that racists hate Muslims as well, not just different coloured skin. But it is the hatred of the obvious – the colour of your skin – which we should concentrate on because the hatred of the hidden – i.e. one's faith and internally held beliefs – is very much a secondary matter and less pressing. Of course, Muslims wear that inner faith very much on the outside and thus like the Jewish community we both suffer from such attacks, at the same time, in a greater proportion. But that shouldn't make us lose focus on the bigger battle of concentrating on the evil of racism in any which way we can.

'By focusing on racism as our priority, we might be able to cover both bases in one swoop'

This article was really just to bring the attention of the Muslims to the bigger fight. Many of our fellow citizens understand this issue far better than we do and indeed perhaps the best article of this year was exactly on this issue, i.e. how we must combat racism in every way possible, when it occurs in every which way it does. And one of these ways, despite the huge blow to its credibility that the Press Complaints Commission has previously suffered, is by actually mentally trying to forget those old days and remember that they are under new management as such after their overhaul as part of the Leveson Inquiry and have shown their seriousness apparently in trying to fix up.

30 July 2012

⇨ The above information is reprinted with kind permission from 1st Ethical. Please visit www.1stethical.com for further information.

Met chief: 'I can't be sure we're not institutionally racist'

Information from the Brixton Blog.

By Tim Dickens, co-editor

London's top police officer told Brixton residents last night that he 'can't be sure' the Metropolitan Police is not racist.

Speaking at Lambeth College, Clapham Common Southside, last night Commissioner Bernard Hogan-Howe responded to questions from residents and community leaders including Brixton Splash chairman Lee Jasper.

He was there to set out his view of 'total policing' before answering a series of questions from the audience.

Jasper, a former equalities advisor to the Mayor of London, accused the Met of a 'resurgent and rampant' level of institutionalised racism. He asked Hogan-Howe: 'Do you accept that your relationship with black communities is in deep crisis? Because I can tell you that is the case.'

Hogan-Howe replied: 'I can only say that I hope we're not, but I can't be sure we're not institutionally racist.'

The police boss faced a barrage of questions about racism in the police, with a number of references made to the mobile phone recording which emerged of a police officer allegedly racially abusing a suspect in the back of a police van in Newham during the August riots.

In response to another question about cameras in police vehicles, Hogan-Howe said: 'We will do that. There's a lot of work to do before it will happen, but it will happen. I can't give you a date today.'

On the subject of stop and search the Commissioner said: 'We've got too many kids being stopped without having done anything. I am not sure we have given

[police officers] enough training for what can be a complicated event. We will probably see fewer stops.'

Marcia Rigg, whose brother Sean Rigg died in custody at Brixton Police station in August 2008, was also at the meeting. She was unhappy that the Commissioner had failed to keep a promise to meet with her following alleged police brutality at a march in central London by the United Families and Friends Campaign in October last year.

Hogan-Howe responded that he would meet with Rigg and her colleagues, but had to wait until the complaint procedure had been closed.

Brixton Splash founder Ros Griffiths and former policewoman and equalities activist Marlene Ellis also asked questions of Hogan-Howe around the subject of race and the police's relationship with black and ethnic minorities.

A number of others who wanted to speak were left disappointed, however, when the chairman brought the meeting to a close at 8.30pm last night.

12 April 2012

⇨ The above information is reprinted with kind permission from the Brixton Blog. Please visit www brixtonblog.com for further information.

Police racism: 293 cases, five dismissals

As the CPS recommends a Met Police officer is charged for racially abusing a suspect during last year's riots, Channel 4 News can exclusively reveal the number of cases of racism among UK police.

The incidents range from racist language in emails to the use of the n***** word.

The figures, obtained under the Freedom of Information Act, date back to the Macpherson report 13 years ago which followed the death of black teenager Stephen Lawrence and led to the Met Police being labelled 'institutionally racist'.

Also on Tuesday, a review by the Crown Prosecution Service (CPS) found 'sufficient evidence' to charge Met Police officer Alex McFarlane with a 'racially aggravated public order offence', and has now advised the Independent Police Complaints Commission (IPCC) to press charges.

The officer was accused of using racist language against a 21-year-old black man, and was apparently recorded by the suspect on his mobile phone.

Earlier this month, Channel 4 News revealed 120 race cases inside the Met and just one dismissal during the same time frame. This data, gathered from 31 forces in England, Scotland, Wales and Northern Ireland, completes the national picture.

Channel 4 News can reveal that between 1999 and 2012:

⇨ 293 police officers were disciplined for racist behaviour

⇨ 749 were referred to the IPCC

⇨ Five were dismissed

⇨ Seven were forced to resign.

Of all the 749 cases referred to the IPCC, 513 were within the Metropolitan Police.

One of the officers who was dismissed in 1999, used insulting and abusive language to another police officer, saying: 'Michael, that's why we keep down n******.' The officer was disciplined by being forced to resign, but on appeal, was dismissed.

Another officer from the same police force was reported in 2006, for interrupting a briefing about treating members of the community equally. He stood up and said: 'Bollocks! They're all black bastards and I hate them all.' The case was not referred to the IPCC and the PC was given a warning.

In many of the cases, officers were fined or given a written warning for inappropriate racist behaviour. One was fined for sending an email including 'inappropriate and racist terminology' from the police server.

Prosecution 'is necessary'

In a statement following her review of PC McFarlane's case, Alison Saunders, Chief Crown Prosecutor said: 'I have taken the decision in this case that, as well as there being sufficient evidence...a prosecution is necessary in order to maintain confidence in the criminal justice system.

'It is regrettable that the original decision was wrong, but I hope the action taken and my decision today demonstrates the willingness of the CPS to review its decisions independently and swiftly and to take appropriate action where necessary.'

The decision comes as Scotland Yard confirmed last week that ten cases are being referred to the Independent Police Complaints Commission (IPCC) after fresh allegations of racist comments earlier this year.

17 April 2012

⇨ A version of this article was first published at channel4.com/news. Please visit www.channel4.com.

Confronting indirect racism

Information from About Equal Opportunities.

By Beth Morrisey

Racism, or the belief that one race is superior to other races, can take many forms. Direct racism occurs when something obvious and blatant is said or done, while indirect racism occurs when something subtle or covert occurs. This 'hidden nature' makes indirect racism very hard to identify sometimes, and even harder to challenge. Refusal to engage, benign ignorance, jokes and banter and imitations and mockery are all types of indirect racism, but all can and should be challenged just as long as you remain safe while doing so.

'Indirect racism occurs when something subtle or covert occurs'

Confronting indirect racism: refusal to engage

Refusal to engage is a type of indirect racism in which others treat an individual of a certain race as an object rather than an individual. This may mean staring at the person, making comments to each other about the person, remaining silent around the person, looking past or through the person or otherwise engaging in behaviours that devalue the person. These behaviours are often calculated to make the individual feel like, at the very least, an outsider. Challenging such instances of refusal to engage can be as easy as introducing yourself and forcing a conversation or otherwise drawing attention to the unacceptable behaviours. If these tactics do not help then ignoring the behaviours and joining another group for small talk might be an easier way to get through an event.

Confronting indirect racism: benign ignorance

'Benign ignorance' is a term that can be applied to behaviours others believe to be helpful or complimentary but do not understand are actually hurtful and degrading. Usually such behaviours or comments are well-intentioned, and the person responsible may even believe that they are paying someone a compliment, but because their words and actions are predicated on stereotypes or prejudice this is not actually the case. When you are faced with an example of benign ignorance, don't be afraid to let the other person know why his or her assumptions make you uncomfortable. Simply saying something like 'Thank you, but I believe my abilities are due to my studies and talents rather than my race' is a polite way to confront the issue but keep the conversation as cordial as possible at the same time.

Confronting indirect racism: jokes and banter

Jokes and banter can be a hard form of indirect racism to challenge because those involved tend to claim 'But I was just joking!' or 'It was just a bit of fun!' Use this excuse to let the perpetrators know why you didn't find something funny, or why it wasn't fun for you to have to listen to their thoughtless words. Of course, this tactic works best if you were not joining in the jokes and banter at any point and it may be that you need to be willing to agree to disagree on the actual meaning of a joke. If nothing else, strive to get everyone involved to agree to avoid racist jokes and banter in the future even if you can't get them to understand why you haven't found their previous words and behaviours all that amusing.

Confronting indirect racism: imitations and mockery

Much like jokes and banter, imitations and outright mockery are often defended as just a bit of fun. Even when someone point out that imitating an accent o mannerism, particularly attributin stereotypical characteristics t someone who does not show ther him or herself, might be hurtfu those engaged in this behaviou often defend themselves by sayin that they didn't mean anything b it or by countering that the perso who was offended was just overl sensitive. These excuses can b deflected by letting people kno that even if they didn't mea anything by it, whether they thin you are too sensitive or not, yo were still hurt. You may ultimatel feel that it's unfair for you to hav to take some responsibility for you honest opinion, but by keepin the focus on how you are feelin, you might be able to have a bette discussion about the impact o their behaviour.

'Jokes and banter can be a hard form of indirect racism to challenge'

Indirect racism can be hard t challenge because those wh engage in it may not even be awar of what they are doing. Refusal t engage, benign ignorance, joke and banter and imitations and mockery are all forms of indirec racism that can and should b confronted.

15 September 2012

⇨ The above information is reprinted with kind permission from About Equa Opportunities. Please visi www.aboutequalopportunities co.uk for further information.

Can you excuse casual racism?

Davina Hamilton questions whether ambiguous race-related incidents can ever be ignored.

Last week, my husband took the morning off work to wait for an engineer, who was due to arrive at our home between 8am and midday (you know they can never give a specific time). Upon arrival, the engineer – a white, middle-aged man – soon proved himself to be one of the chatty ones, talking to my other half as if he'd known him for years.

Many black people are often wary of crying racism, for fear that they'll be accused of 'playing the race card'

The workman then asked my spouse how he liked the area, before telling him: 'Yeah, I used to like it round here, but then all the fighting started between the blacks and the Greeks.'

When my husband – who is black – relayed this story to me, I was unsure of what to say or how to feel. I just couldn't seem to find the appropriate emotion. Part of me wanted to laugh at the sheer tactlessness of the engineer, while another part of me wondered whether the man was a casual racist.

Was the ethnicity of the alleged troublemakers really that important to mention, especially to a black man? If the alleged fighting had been between groups of white boys, would the engineer have stated this when sharing his feelings about the area?

I asked friends what they made of the scenario. Some were in no doubt that the man was racist; others thought he was just relaying a fact; and some felt he was simply tactless to say that to a black man. I remained unsure.

Many black people are often wary of crying racism, for fear that they'll be accused of 'playing the race card'. Meanwhile, others are quick to find racism in situations where, perhaps, there is none. But with much of today's racial prejudice being far less overt than it was in years gone by (the days of hotel doors featuring the infamous 'no blacks, no Irish, no dogs' signs are, thankfully, behind us), racism is often not as black and white as it once was.

Now, on occasion, incidents like the chatty engineer's 'blacks and Greeks' comment, leave us unsure of whether seemingly innocent remarks hide casual racism. And without knowing for sure, should such incidents be brushed under the carpet?

Think back to last year when Naomi Campbell accused Cadbury of racism. In an advertising campaign for a new chocolate bar, the confectionery giant went with the strapline, 'Move over Naomi, there's a new diva in town.' To put it mildly, the supermodel was not best pleased, accusing Cadbury of being racist by likening black people to chocolate.

Some black people were in full support of Naomi's complaint. Recalling the type of racism that took place in English schools of yesteryear, where black children were teased about their skin looking like chocolate, many felt that Cadbury was indeed racist to liken a black model to a chocolate bar.

But then there were those who rubbished the cries of racism, firmly believing that Cadbury was referencing Campbell's diva reputation and not her skin colour.

So when it's impossible to prove whether or not an incident is racist, should we be up in arms about it?

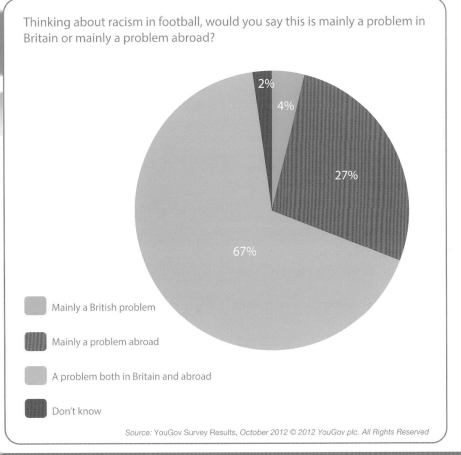

Thinking about racism in football, would you say this is mainly a problem in Britain or mainly a problem abroad?

- 2%
- 4%
- 27%
- 67%

- Mainly a British problem
- Mainly a problem abroad
- A problem both in Britain and abroad
- Don't know

Source: YouGov Survey Results, October 2012 © 2012 YouGov plc. All Rights Reserved

I had similar thoughts upon hearing another story recently from one of my friends (another black man).

He told me that he had decided to leave his job as a city broker, after being told by his boss (a white man) that the company thought it best not to send a black man to do a particular job.

'Sometimes, towards the end of the month, the company used to send junior brokers to clients' houses to get cheques,' recalled my friend, who chose to remain anonymous. 'It's fairly normal for small investment houses and it increases that particular month's revenue.

'I was all set to go when my line manager came over, looking sheepish, as if he wasn't sure what to say. Then, another supervisor – though not the main boss – came over and told me that the boss "doesn't want to send a black guy to one of the clients". Apparently, they thought that a black guy turning up at the client's house might "shock him".

'They basically decided it would reflect badly on the company somehow, and so told me not to go. I was so angry that I decided to leave my job at the end of that month.'

What was interesting about my friend's saga was that his supervisor didn't think my friend had any cause to be offended by the company boss's decision.

'When it's impossible to prove whether or not an incident is racist, should we be up in arms about it?'

'He wasn't even a little bit bothered when he told me what the boss had decided. In fact, I think he felt like I should have been more understanding about the potential racism of an old man.'

Here lies my issue. While I was disgusted to hear what my friend had been through – and was in no doubt that he was the victim of

racism – it got me wondering if any racism can be 'justified'.

When it comes from an old, white Englishman, who grew up as part of a generation where such racism was deemed fair game, should we be surprised?

When a middle-aged white woman in a restaurant a few years ago asked me where I was from and I replied 'London', and she retorted, 'no, where are you really from?', was she just curious, downright ignorant, or attempting to make me feel that while I may have been born in England, it's not really 'my' country?

When shop assistants coincidentally find the need to 'tidy up' every area of the shop that a black customer happens to stop at, are they just doing their job, or indirectly insinuating that black people are prone to stealing?

Last year, a black American teenager filmed a white man, assumed to be a shop assistant, who kept following him in a store. In the video, which was posted on YouTube, viewers see the man appearing behind the teen every time he turns a corner.

It certainly seems that the young man, who is shopping with his friend, is being followed. And

with the video titled 'Racist gu[y] following us', it's clear the tee[n] believes he is a victim of racism.

'Racism today comes i[n] many different guise[s] and very often it'[s] hard to prove['

But unlike the unquestionabl[e] racist intent of a white perso[n] calling a black person a 'n****r[', this type of incident (which man[y] of us have experienced whils[t] shopping), is much harder to prov[e] as being an act of racism.

The fact is, racism today come[s] in many different guises an[d] very often it's hard to prove. S[o] when the motive, the reason o[r] the thinking behind incidents o[f] potential racism is unclear, shoul[d] those incidents be challenged o[r] just shrugged off?

4 February 2012

⇨ The above information i[s] reprinted with kind permissio[n] from *The Voice*. Please visi[t] www.voice-online.co.uk fo[r] further information.

Online racism

Law targets racism on social networking sites.

By Nick Branch

A spate of recent cases has highlighted the disturbing amount of racism on social networking sites such as Twitter, prompting celebrities and footballers to quit the medium and sparking a debate on how racism can be tackled online.

Recent cases include that of a student who was jailed after posting a racist comment about the collapsed Bolton midfielder, Fabrice Muamba. Another similar case involved a student at Newcastle University. Joshua Cryer, 21, admitted using the social networking site to post racist abuse about the former Liverpool striker, Stan Collymore.

The Crown Prosecution Service is using a variety of laws to bring these foul-mouthed bigots to justice. Joshua Cryer was charged under section 127 of the Communications Act, for sending grossly offensive messages, including racist taunts, to Collymore. He was sentenced to a two-year community order, 240 hours community service and ordered to pay £150 costs.

The case concerning Fabrice Muamba was perhaps even more striking given the condition of the Bolton midfielder and the public outpouring of support for him and his family. Liam Stacey, a 21-year-old Biology student at Swansea University was charged with making racially aggravated comments about him as he lay fighting for his life. He is due for sentencing this week, and has been warned that he could face a custodial sentence for his remarks.

Prosecutors are keen to ensure that events which take place online are treated with the same force as those which occur in public. Legal action is easier to pursue as online accounts can be traced, and evidence is automatically held on servers. Faced with this, offenders usually plead guilty, avoiding any significant police involvement with the case.

Wendy Williams is the head of the Crown Prosecution Service in the north-east.

'In recent months we have seen a number of similar cases in the north-east, in which people have been racially abused through social networking sites. Ironically, the strongest evidence in each of these cases has been directly provided by the defendants themselves,' she said.

'When a person makes such comments digitally, they effectively hand police and prosecutors much of the evidence needed to build a robust case against them,' she added.

28 March 2012

⇨ Information from FindLawUK. Please visit blogs.findlaw.co.uk for further information.

© FindLawUK

Jail for student in Muamba Twitter race rant a perversion of justice

S wansea student Liam Stacey has been sentenced to 56 days for a 'racially aggravated public order offence' after tweeting a very poor taste joke about footballer Fabrice Muamba followed by several racist and inflammatory comments.

The 21-year-old claimed he had been drinking all day and was quite drunk by the time he'd sent tweets. This is most likely true. It was St Patrick's Day and the last day of the Six Nations rugby championship, and quite a lot of people would have spent that day in the pub. But while it may be true, it's hardly a defence.

Is Stacey a racist? A troll? A drunk and mouthy young man? Possibly a little of each. But none of these are illegal. Stacey's conviction is for a public order offence.

One can understand why public order laws exist. The police may need to be able to take people off the streets to prevent imminent violence, and be able to punish people for causing disruptions.

But was there actually any risk that Stacey was threatening public order? I don't think there was. A row on Twitter is not the same thing as shouting abuse in the street, where there may be immediate physical consequences. Twitter may be like a pub, in the sense that it's a space for social interaction, but it's definitely not the pub in that when tempers fray, no one's going to get glassed. The worst that will happen is someone will block you.

Only one of Stacey's tweets was violent in nature, and that did not contain any racial abuse. So has he been jailed for eight weeks solely for being offensive at a time when people on Twitter were congratulating themselves for the outpouring of goodwill to the fallen Muamba? If so, then people who care about free expression should be very, very worried.

27 March 2012

⇨ Information from Index on Censorship. Please visit blog.indexoncensorship.org.

© 1997-2012 Index on Censorship

Are East Europeans victims of racism in the UK?

Information from the University of Bristol.

Since 2004, nearly 1.9 million East Europeans have come to the UK. New research, led by academics at the University of Bristol, has examined how current East European migration to the UK has been racialised in immigration policy and tabloid journalism, providing the first insights into how racism is affecting migrants' experiences of work and life in the UK.

In an 18-month project, published in the journal *Sociology*, led by Dr Jon Fox, Senior Lecturer from the University's School of Sociology, Politics and International Studies, researchers explored questions of racism surrounding Hungarian and Romanian migration to the UK.

The evidence to date from the UK suggests that shared 'whiteness' offers few protections against racism. Like earlier generations of Irish migrants to the UK and USA, East European Jews a century ago, and more recently East European Roma, this new generation of East European migrant workers has been subjected to various forms of racism, racial discrimination and racial stigmatisation.

This is not the crude racisms of epithets and insults; rather, it is the racialisation of innuendo and inference.

Dr Fox, lead author of the study, said: 'Our analyses found that shared whiteness between migrant and majority has not exempted these migrants from the sorts of racialisation found in other migrations.' The study examined immigration policy and the tabloid media for evidence of different forms of racialisation.

'Hungarians [who like Poles were not subject to immigration control] have benefited from an immigration policy that whilst motivated by economic considerations, was underlined by racialised preferences. Romanians, in contrast, were subjected to strict immigration controls, not because they didn't match the preferred racial profile of migrants, but because concern over their numbers trumped both economic and racialised rationales for letting in more migrants.

'While immigration controls against Romanians were not racially motivated, they did produce racialised effects. Romanians were symbolically stripped of their whiteness by an immigration policy that refused to recognise them as full Europeans with associated rights.'

In the tabloid media, in contrast, it was the Romanians who received the bulk of (negative) attention. This is because Romanians, unlike Hungarians, stepped into an unfolding narrative of stigmatisation that reached back to post-Ceauescu images of AIDS babies supposedly fraudulent asylum claims, and a host of unsavoury activities ranging from begging and prostitution to petty theft and smuggling. Associations with the Roma and gypsy/travellers in the UK cemented their negative reputation in the tabloid press' handling of the current migrations.

The study's findings show how two cohorts of migrants neighbours in East Europe and phenotypically indistinguishable from one another (and indeed from a white British majority), are dramatically lightened and darkened by immigration policy and the tabloid media.

Dr Fox added: 'Our analyses reveal how immigration policy and the tabloid media have contributed to the whitening and darkening of Hungarian and Romanian migrants. Immigration policy whitened Hungarian migrants; the tabloid media darkened Romanian migrants.'

The study, entitled *The racialisation of the new European migration to the UK*, was funded by the Economic and Social Research Council (ESRC).

21 August 2012

⇨ The above information is reprinted with kind permission from the University of Bristol. Please visit www.bris.ac.uk for further information.

One in three Brits admits they are racist

Information from OnePoll.

One in three Brits admits they are racist. A third admitted regularly making comments or being involved in discussions which could be considered racist and more than one in ten admitted they had been accused of being a racist by someone close to them. Furthermore, almost 40 per cent confessed to using the phrase 'I'm not a racist, but ...' when discussing race issues facing Britain today.

These worrying figures emerged through a OnePoll survey of 2,000 adults who were asked to honestly express their feelings about foreign nationals living and working in this country.

Alarmingly, many felt their animosity towards foreigners was passed down by previous generations. But the country's immigration policy also emerged as a trigger for emotions which could be considered racist.

The true extent of the racist undercurrent within the country was revealed in this nationally representative study in which 88 per cent of the respondents classed themselves as 'White British'.

What constitutes being racist will always be a contentious issue, with what one person deems inappropriate the next person may not. Likewise, life experience and cultures we have grown-up in are inevitably going to influence our beliefs and the language we use.

The study also found one in five accept the fact that people around them make disparaging remarks about different ethnic groups – and are not bothered by it.

Age-wise, the over-55s were found to have the biggest chips on their shoulders, with the 18-24 age range close behind. The younger of these two brackets were also more likely to admit making racist comments or partaking in behaviour which could be deemed racist.

The Government's immigration policy was slammed by many of those who took part in the study. 71 per cent said they felt the 'open doors' approach to foreign nationals was leading to an increase in racist feelings. As many as one in six demanded Britain close its doors to anyone who is not a UK national.

It's alarming that so many people are just accepting the racist behaviour around them. The findings did show that immigration policy was fuelling the fire for racist behaviour amongst some adults. However, immigration and race are two separate issues although these findings show that many believe one is a consequence of another.

30 May 2012

⇨ The above information is reprinted with kind permission from OnePoll. Please visit www.onepoll.com for further information.

Blackness is not a costume

... and other facts you should know.

By Helen Gould

The President of the University of Birmingham Christian Union, Ben McNeely, was recently caught 'blacking up' to fit a 'Caribbean' theme for a fancy dress party. BEMA, the Birmingham Ethnic Minorities Association, found the photograph posted on Facebook (it was later deleted by McNeely) and fortunately succeeded in convincing him of the severity of the situation.

McNeely has made a public apology, and will be resigning as President of the Christian Union. He says that he had no 'intention to offend' and 'was genuinely unaware of the history attached to this issue.'

As many black people could tell him, intent is not magic. If I 'accidentally' punch someone in the face, and then say I didn't mean to break their nose, that doesn't heal them. Similarly, if you treat a skin colour like an accessory, saying you didn't mean to do any harm does not atone for the damage you have done. Thankfully, he has done the right thing; but his claim to have no knowledge about the history of blacking up is simply astounding.

Yet he is not the only one. An article in the *Birmingham Mail* was posted to the UK section of the popular website Reddit where it gained almost 300 comments. The most upvoted comment there asked, 'Maybe I'm missing something, but is this really bad?' Others doubting how 'bad' blackface is, and attempting to defend the act of blacking up, quickly followed:

'I had a friend black up for Halloween and go as Samuel L. Jackson from *Pulp Fiction*. Is that racist? I don't particularly think so...'

'This guy was clearly just having fun. How else would you impersonate a black person if not by blacking up?'

'Is no-one is allowed to dress up as someone outside their race? That seems kinda racist in itself.'

And of course, the inevitable:

'Oh look, it's the PC police.'

The thread continues, with some other Redditors attempting to enlighten these people as to why blackface is at best a sensitive subject and at worst downright insulting. The following information will hopefully be helpful to the people in that thread – and perhaps even some who are reading this article right now – who are baffled that a black person might react badly to seeing their skin colour worn as an accessory.

Blackface and the imagery of blackface was used for years to dehumanise, ridicule and stereotype black people in the USA and Britain. It led to many of the harmful stereotypes that still exist today – the Mammy stereotype, for instance, which portrays black women as perpetual domestic servants, servile and happy to be so, permanently good-natured and endlessly nurturing to the white families they served. It was first used as a subtle defence of slavery – a version of the 'happy slave' myth. You may recognise this fabrication from films like *Gone with the Wind* and *The Help*. There is also the more general stereotype of black people being stupid, uneducated, and worthy of derision; this can be seen in any of the old popular minstrel shows.

Blackface was used all the way up to 1981, when the sitcom *Are You Being Served?* had an episode that ended in a minstrel routine. In fact, the argument could be made that it has never stopped being used; comedian Billy Crystal darkened his skin in order to do an impression of Sammy Davis Jr. at the Oscars earlier this year, and Ashton Kutcher used it in a commercial for Popchips.

It is easy to tell another person not to be offended about something because you personally think that you wouldn't mind. Similar things are often said when it comes to other social issues – statements along the lines of 'I wouldn't be offended if someone told me I looked nice on the street!', for instance. It almost always comes from people who do not actually have to deal with the problem, whether it is racism, sexism, homophobia, or any other bigoted attitude. And to those people, it must be said that you don't know how it feels and you have no right to tell another person how to feel. You have little basis for your opinion when the issue does not apply to you and you have never experienced it. It is like sitting in a well-insulated house in the winter, and telling someone shivering outside that you don't think it's that cold. You don't have to deal with the snow.

Each time a white person is oblivious or racist enough to use blackface to portray a black person, they reinforce a hurtful narrative used for racist reasons and with an incredibly harmful history; a history that contributed to the oppression of ethnic minorities and helped deny our humanity.

And remember, 'I didn't know' only works once.

18 October 2012

⇨ The above information is reprinted with kind permission from *The Student Journals*. Please visit www.studentjournals.co.uk for further information.

Free speech: Are we getting the balance right?

You spoke out and told us your views.

Striking the right balance between protecting people's right to speak freely, while also promoting respect, sensitivity and tolerance, seems to be a perpetual issue in the UK and other liberal democracies.

YouGov's PoliticsLab invited you to speak out and tell us your views on freedom of speech:

Has society become too politically correct and oversensitive? OR are too many people still making racist, sexist and homophobic comments that need clamping down on?

⇨ The largest proportion of those who took part in the debate were of the opinion that political correctness has gone too far in Britain, to the detriment of public debate, and that both regular people and the media have become overly sensitive.

⇨ A smaller proportion of participants said that too many people are still making offensive remarks against certain groups, and that the right to freedom of speech should not be used to evade accountability for inciting hatred.

⇨ A very small proportion of you said you thought the balance was about right. Those who were of this view, said that while there are extreme examples on both sides, it is a natural tension in a modern democracy that is managed fairly well in Britain.

So what sort of things did participants say on this subject?

Below we look at the two opposite views represented most in this discussion.

VIEWPOINT: 'Society has become too easily offended towards people making politically incorrect comments'

⇨ Those of you who argued that the idea of political correctness has gone too far, said it stifles what could be constructive debate on important issues.

⇨ You also said that a culture of fear has taken hold, where people feel nervous about saying what is on their minds because people are too easily offended and eager to label someone as prejudiced.

Argument 1 – Political correctness stifles debate

'"Political correctness" is being used to marginalise minority views in society, and by political and media elites to enforce consensus by socially stigmatising those who have alternative perspectives, in the name of tolerance.' Anon

'A society that dismisses the thoughts and opinions of any sector of its public is one which is unhealthy. Also, we have got to the stage where the only sector of the population able to be discriminated against or laughed at is the white male.' Anon

'Attempting to censor insulting comments will not get rid of them, but drive them underground and keep the underlying attitudes hidden. Allowing all the freedom to insult others is the best way to expose the hateful attitudes of some, and challenge them rather than let them hide and go unchallenged.' A. Williams, Teesside

'Every day there are stories in the news of people complaining that a radical extremist has made another outrageous statement. Let them speak their mind and let their words be the means by which we can decide if they should be followed, respected or ignored.' Ray, Somerset

'How can issues be debated if we can't discuss sensitive issues? I'm not talking about people being aggressively phobic towards a group of people, but people just making controversial comments. If someone is offended then the only way to solve this is by discussion and education, not pretending people don't think in certain ways.' Anon

'I think that political correctness is preventing people from even raising certain subjects, i.e. immigration, let alone discussing them. Freedom of speech will inevitably displease some people, and especially those who make a career out of being offended.' Geoffrey, Hertfordshire

Argument 2 – Political correctness has created a culture of fear where too many are unfairly labelled as bigots

'I am retired and 70 years old. In my lifetime laws and rules have changed and we are expected to put a lifetime of taught beliefs behind us in an instant … Beliefs are to some extent ingrained, and while acceptance is expected it can be difficult to adjust. So the slip of the tongue, while not intended to hurt or belittle, is now a case for every lawyer and politician to ride on the wagon.' Anon

'Children in schools just have to mention the race issue and they can get away with anything because teachers live in fear of being called a racist. This is stupid. Most people are not racist, or sexist, or anything else. Stop wrongly accusing people because of obviously innocent remarks. Our freedom of speech has been taken away from us. That is far more fascist than the regime these rules have been set up to prevent.' Ashley, Nottingham

'Every day is like walking on eggshells; some people take great pleasure in sniffing out, and being allegedly offended at others' views. For this reason it inhibits social interaction; I've actually given up talking to some people because of it. The last Government's decision to redefine this area was the most significant decision: they allowed racism to become entirely subjective … Anyone can become a criminal based on the sensibilities of others.' Philip, Plymouth

'There is a smug, complacent, soggy, left-of-centre middle that is rapidly becoming the only acceptable position to hold on anything. It is the tyranny of the illiberal liberal. Much of the time accepted truth is utterly false. We pretend reality is not as it is in the name of faux politeness.' Blognorton

'I encounter things which deeply offend me on an almost daily basis, but there's no law or bleeding hearts to stop them. Being offended by things is part of life, and the minorities whose delicate sensibilities the liberals claim are offended should get over it. After all, people who can still be called an "old hag", "ugly", "stupid", "boring", etc., have to live with such things without collapsing into a state and going to court.' Anon

'My next door neighbour is an 86-year-old staunch racist; she is a product of her time and has led a sheltered "rich white" life. We often have great discussions, and although I may not agree with all she says her views are valid and show just how much society has changed. No-one likes change, and in her lifetime she has seen the demographics, race, creed, and rights of all these people overtake her own. Rightly so, she feels outnumbered in her own country and due to her age has no qualms in voicing this opinion. This is free speech at its best because she is entitled to her opinion and we should respect it.' Daz, Cheshire

VIEWPOINT: 'Too many people still making racist, sexist and homophobic comments'

⇨ Those who argued that there is still too much racism, sexism and homophobia in society, said that people who make offensive remarks should be more harshly criticised, and held to account for what they've said.

⇨ You also told us that the right to freedom of speech should not act as a shield for those who incite hatred, including anonymously online, and that in some cases people making offensive comments should be prosecuted.

Argument 1 – People need to be held accountable for what they say

'Despite our country being incredibly multicultural, there are still those who make remarks that can lead to ignorance and bigoted intolerance of others. These views must be reprimanded, and those who make them educated about why such intolerance is unfounded. To ignore such views is not an option in this society.' Olly M., Newquay

'Even if a comment is not aimed directly at an individual, the words still hurt, and cause misery and pain. Pulling people up on their bigoted comments draws attention to this very serious problem in our society.' Nicola E., London

'I think that when you have groups of Muslim extremists shouting hate at soldiers returning from service in Afghanistan, they should not only be criticised for it but punished for treason. Likewise, when there are groups of white skinheads screaming at Muslim women, they should not only be criticised but punished for inciting racial hatred.' Anon

'Of course people should be criticised for making offensive comments. Anyone saying "political correctness has gone too far" has clearly never been on the receiving end of bigotry and is deeply lacking any sense of empathy.' Anon

'The recent Rio Ferdinand fiasco illustrates this really well. John Terry is the one in the penalty box for allegedly making racist remarks, or is he? Rio is the one left out of the England squad while Terry's trial is delayed so he can take part in Euro2012, and when Rio expresses that this is unfair he is tagged as the problem by some pretty strongly opinionated people who claim he has proven that he would have been a troublemaker if included … It seems you can say whatever you like that is offensive and almost the entire nation will become your defence, if only to stress that there is no racism in the UK, and those who feel they have been discriminated against are too keen to play the race card.' Natsai Z., Nottingham

'There shouldn't be any legal restrictions on what people say, but there should be more, louder, harder and specific criticism of people when they do say things that promote or maintain negative treatment or consideration of particular groups … This is the responsibility of every individual, and shouldn't be delegated just to the media or other institutions.' Anon

Argument 2 – People should not be able to hide behind freedom of speech

'Racism, sexism and homophobia are irrational and divisive and generally such comments are not made in any sort of active discussion, but in simple negation. Freedom of speech is not and should not be an absolute right.' Malcolm, Frome

'Free speech is overrated. In the dreadful world of tweeting and texting, any notion of responsibility for one's actions seems to have disappeared. As a consequence, some curtailment of this supposed "freedom" is inevitable – and absolutely necessary.' Anon

'Simply making a comment then hiding behind freedom of speech or religion to defend themselves or shield themselves from criticism is at odds with the principle.' Lei, Wales

'With the rise of social media, particularly Twitter, people seem to be losing touch with personal accountability and too many offensive comments are made with no expectation of repercussion. Extremist politics have 'lso been frighteningly prevalent globally in the last few years, and sending a strong zero-tolerance message about offensive language and behaviour may discourage others from partaking in it.' Emily P., Scotland

'Certain subjects should be off-limits, when the person being laughed at or criticised is a victim of a crime or has some kind of disability or impairment in particular.' Anon

'People are actively seeking out groups they can safely victimise in order to boost their own fading sense of self-worth. Until we can stop this drive to find people to victimise then we should continue to push the message that bullying and verbal assault is a crime.' Dee D., Yorkshire

15 June 2012

⇨ The above information is reprinted with kind permission from YouGov. Please visit www.yougov. co.uk for further information.

A message from British National Party leader Nick Griffin MEP

Information from the British National Party.

Fellow British Patriot

The BNP is a patriotic, democratic alternative to the old parties that have wrecked our great country.

Native British are now treated like second-class citizens in our own country, whilst asylum-seekers and immigrants are pushed to the front of the queue for housing, jobs and benefits.

Millions of our people are unemployed yet the politicians continue to allow foreign workers to flood into Britain, taking our jobs or claiming benefits, costing us billions of pounds.

While we struggle to pay the bills and live in fear of losing our jobs, the crooked politicians are fiddling their expenses and stealing taxpayers' money.

Whilst the politicians lavish billions on undeserving foreigners and mega-rich bankers, thousands of our pensioners freeze to death every winter, or are forced to eke out a miserable existence on tiny pensions.

Despite the huge sacrifice of millions of our war heroes to keep our country free and independent, the politicians have sold us out to the European Union, taking away our right to rule ourselves and decide our own laws.

Towns and cities all over our beautiful country now resemble parts of Africa or Asia. British people have become a minority in many areas already, and within a few decades, we will become a minority across the country as a whole.

Almost every day now, a brave British soldier is brought back from Afghanistan in a coffin. Our boys and girls are sent to fight a war that has nothing to do with Britain or British interests. Despite the illegal war in Afghanistan, Muslim extremism is flourishing on the streets of Britain.

What would our War Heroes think if they could see Britain today? They fought to keep this country British. They fought to keep our nation free, sovereign and independent. They did not fight for multiculturalism, political correctness, or to see our country flooded with foreigners and our own people made into second-class citizens.

Where we stand:

⇨ We will put British people first in their own country,

⇨ We demand British jobs go to British workers,

⇨ We say NO to an EU superstate, and YES to keeping Britain free,

⇨ We will stop paying foreign aid and give that money to pensioners,

⇨ and we will bring British troops home from Afghanistan.

Enough is enough! The BNP is the only genuine alternative to the old parties, that's why the media lies about us all the time.

We don't care about the nasty names the media liars and politicians call us; we love our country and our children, and we are proud to be British.

Ring the following number for a free information pack:

0844 809 4581

Yours faithfully,

Nick Griffin MEP

Leader, British National Party

⇨ The above information is reprinted with kind permission from the British National Party. Please visit www.bnp.org.uk for further information.

Racism kicked out of football? Not yet

While the FA's stance has improved, more still needs to be done to address any form of racial discrimination in football.

By Musa Okwonga

The issue of racism in football is alive and well. Mark McCammon, a professional footballer, has successfully brought a case for racial victimisation against Gillingham, his former club. McCammon, who is black, was found by an employment tribunal to have been unfairly dismissed due to his race: this finding in his favour is the first of its type in English law.

Elsewhere, the issue is alive too. The FA has charged Chelsea's John Terry with the alleged use of abusive and/or insulting words and/or behaviour towards Queens Park Rangers' Anton Ferdinand. This comes, of course, after Terry was found not guilty of racially abusing Ferdinand in a criminal trial. More recently, the FA has also charged Rio Ferdinand, Anton's brother, with acting 'in a way which was improper and/or brought the game into disrepute by making comments which included a reference to ethnic origin and/or colour and/or race' after he retweeted and laughed at a comment referring to Ashley Cole, the Chelsea and England defender, as a 'choc ice'.

Some might say this is minor compared with what McCammon suffered at Gillingham (which, incidentally, is due to appeal against the tribunal's finding). What emerged from the Terry-Ferdinand trial was that, during that match between QPR and Chelsea on 23 October, two grown men had traded insults in a childish spat. Ashley Cole, when called to give evidence, was clearly exasperated. 'We shouldn't be sitting here,' he told the court, and many, having followed the trial closely, would be minded to agree

with him. At this point, we can step back and ask: what have we all learned?

There is nothing much new that has been learned about Anton Ferdinand, save his somewhat unimaginative choice of abuse. There is nothing new we have learned about Terry. The same goes for Rio Ferdinand, although it is strange that a renowned authoritarian such as Sir Alex Ferguson allows one of his players to be so prolific and so vociferous on Twitter. But I think a great deal more has been learned about the FA, and its attitude to racism in football.

This affair has shown the FA in the best of lights, and in the worst. On the plus side, its decision to charge Rio Ferdinand for his conduct on Twitter was sound. Had it done otherwise, it would have been open to the accusation that the only type of racially offensive slur that it found unacceptable was that made by a white person about a black person's skin colour – though Ferdinand has denied that calling Cole 'choc ice' was racist, saying it was actually a reference to him being fake.

While this charge may to some appear trivial, I believe it is consistent. It shows that the FA is determined to be exhaustive in its efforts to address any form of racial discrimination in football.

But on the downside, though Terry was well within his rights to seek a postponement of the trial until after Euro 2012, the FA should have made him unavailable for selection during that time. This would not have foreshadowed his guilt: of course, in any criminal trial the defendant is innocent until proven guilty. Instead, the FA would have shown everyone that the disciplinary process takes priority over everything, including football: which, after all, is just another form of employment, if more glamorous than most. But the FA did not have the bravery to take this opportunity.

There will presumably be several players out there who have suffered racial discrimination in football, and who will anxiously be watching how the FA handles the final stages of this issue. They will be hoping that the FA plods scrupulously and rather more bravely through every stage of the process.

31 July 2012

⇨ The above information originally appeared in *The Guardian* and is reprinted with permission. Please visit www.guardian.co.uk.

Tottenham defend fans over Society of Black Lawyers threat

***Information from* The Huffington Post.**

Tottenham have defended their fans after the Society of Black Lawyers threatened to make a complaint to police over their claims anti-Semitic abuse is taking place at White Hart Lane.

Spurs supporters can regularly be heard chanting 'Yid Army' or affectionately refer to some players as 'Yiddos' as a badge of honour in reference to their large Jewish following.

The society's chair Peter Herbert says there has to be 'zero tolerance' against such songs, but Spurs responded with a statement claiming their followers do not cause any offence' by singing it.

'Our guiding principle in respect of the "Y-word" is based on the point of law itself – the distinguishing factor is the intent with which it is used, i.e. if it is used with the deliberate intention to cause offence,' the club said.

This has been the basis of prosecutions of fans of other teams to date. Our fans adopted the chant as a defence mechanism in order to own the term and thereby deflect anti-Semitic abuse. They do not use the term to others to cause any offence, they use it as a chant amongst themselves.

'The club believes that real anti-Semitic abuse such as hissing to simulate the noise of gas chambers is the real evil and the real offence. We believe this is the area that requires a determined and concerted effort from all parties and where we seek greater support to eradicate.'

Herbert had earlier said: 'It does not make a difference if it is Tottenham fans doing the chants or away fans – if they continue to do it we will report it to the police.

'There has to be zero tolerance and if that catches out Spurs then so be it.'

Asked about Jewish fans themselves singing the chant, he said: 'That's not acceptable either.'

He added: 'If neither Tottenham FC nor the FA are willing to take a stand then SBL will report the matter to the Metropolitan Police Service for investigation and, if necessary, prosecution.'

The group behind the push for a black players' union have also put forward a ten-point plan to combat racism in football.

The society also wants to give referees the power to call off games if there is racial abuse from the terraces and have advised any player guilty of airing a racial insult should be sacked.

7 September 2012

⇨ The above information is from *The Huffington Post* and is reprinted with permission from AOL (UK). Please visit www.huffingtonpost.co.uk for further information.

Key facts

⇨ Under the 1976 Race Relations Act, it is unlawful for a person to discriminate on racial grounds against another person. The Act defines racial grounds as including race, colour, nationality or ethnic or national origins. (page 1)

⇨ Just under half (47%) of people thought that there was more racial prejudice today than five years ago. (page 3)

⇨ Muslim people (17%), Asian people (15%) and Eastern European people (12%) were the groups most likely to be identified as subject to increased racial prejudice. (page 4)

⇨ There are more than four times as many black and ethnic minority MPs in Parliament as there were in 1993. (page 8)

⇨ Black men are 26 times more likely than their white counterparts to be stopped and searched by police, while black men and women in their early twenties are twice as likely to be not in employment, education or training as white people. (page 8)

⇨ The population has changed since 1993: then ethnic minorities accounted for 5.1 per cent in England and Wales; the latest figure is 8.7 per cent. (page 8)

⇨ A Ministry of Justice analysis of tens of thousands of cases found that in 2010, 23 per cent of white defendants were sent to prison for indictable offences, compared with 27 per cent of black counterparts and 29 per cent of Asian defendants. (page 9)

⇨ Just over five per cent of adverts in 2010 used actors from a non-white background, while ethnic minorities represent about 13 per cent of the population. (page 11)

⇨ While black players are a common sight on the pitch, there are hardly any black faces to be seen in club boardrooms – with just two black managers in the entire football league. (page 12)

⇨ 51,187 racist incidents were recorded by the police in 2010/11. (page 13)

⇨ A recent BBC report (2012) looking into racism in schools found nearly 88,000 racist incidents took place in UK schools over a four-year period. (page 15)

⇨ Since 2001, concern about race relations, immigrants or immigration has been an important issue with latest data (from December 2011) showing that with around one in five (22 per cent) of people say it is an important issue. (page 17)

⇨ Researchers from the University of Essex found that in 1993 white people earned an average of 18p an hour more than non-whites, but by 2008 the gap had risen to 43p an hour. This was around 7.5% of the minimum wage for those over 21 in 2008, or 3.6% of median hourly earnings. (page 18)

⇨ 60% of black students do not expect to be in work within six months of graduating and 68% expect to be earning less than £25,000 p.a. in that first graduate role. (page 19)

⇨ The majority of the 15,000 caravans that are homes to gypsy and traveller families in England are on sites provided by local authorities, or which are privately owned with planning permission for this use. But the location and condition of these sites would not be tolerated for any other section of society. 26 per cent are situated next to, or under, motorways, 13 per cent next to runways, 12 per cent are next to rubbish tips and four per cent adjacent to sewage farms. (page 21)

⇨ Channel 4 News can reveal that between 1999 and 2012 293 police officers were disciplined for racist behaviour. (page 27)

⇨ One in three Brits admits they are racist. Age-wise, the over-55s were found to have the biggest chips on their shoulders, with the 18-24 age range close behind. The younger of these two brackets were also more likely to admit making racist comments or partaking in behaviour which could be deemed racist. (page 33)

Discrimination

Unfair treatment of someone because of the group/class they belong to.

Ethnic minority

A group of people who are different in their ancestry, culture and traditions from the majority of the population.

Gypsies and travellers

Gypsies and travellers have traditionally pursue a nomadic lifestyle which involves moving around from place to place. English gypsies and Irish travellers are protected under the Race Relations Act. This is because they are members of a community with a shared history stretching back over hundreds of years and are recognised by the law as a distinct ethnic minority group.

Harassment

A behaviour that is usually persistent and is intended to cause distress and offence.

Islamophobia

An extreme fear and hatred of Islam and people who follow the Islam faith, otherwise known as Muslims. Since the 11 September 2001 terrorist attacks in New York and Washington and the 7/7 London bombings (7 July 2005), there have been a lot of strong, controversial debates surrounding Muslims and Islam. This has provoked unfair stereotyping of Muslims as people associate their faith with extreme terrorist actions.

Racism

The belief that one race is superior to another / behaving in a negative or harmful way to someone because of their race.

Racial discrimination

Racial discrimination occurs when a person is treated less favourably because of their colour, race, nationality or ethnic or national origins.

Racial prejudice

The belief and prejudgment that one race is inferior to another. Feeling hatred towards another race just because they are different.

Reverse discrimination

When trying to address social inequalities, sometimes reverse discrimination occurs. This occurs when discrimination is directed towards the dominant group in society, in order to favour the usually disadvantaged minority group. People sometimes refer to this as "positive discrimination".

Multiculturalism

A number of different cultures coexisting side-by-side, for example within a school or a country.

The Race Relations Act 1976

The Race Relations Act 1976 is concerned with people's actions and the effects of their actions, not their opinions or beliefs. The Act makes it unlawful to racially discriminate against anyone. Racial discrimination is when someone treats a person less favourably because of their colour, race, nationality or ethnic or national origins. Racial discrimination is not the same as racial prejudice. It is not necessary to prove that the other person intended to discriminate against you: you only have to show that you received less favourable treatment as a result of what they did. The Race Relations Act 1976 also aims to promote race equality and good race relations.

Assignments

1. What is racism? Discuss in groups and create a poster to demonstrate your definition. You could use cartoons, images from newspapers or examples you find on the Internet.

2. Research racial discrimination in either the UK, the USA or South Africa. Create a timeline of important events from the last 100 years.

3. Visit the Kick it Out! website (www.kickitout.org) and research their 'Let's kick racism out of football' campaign. Do you think the campaign is working? What else could be done to tackle the issue of racism in football? Perhaps you think that people are over-sensitive about this issue. Write a few short paragraphs explaining your thoughts.

4. What is Islamophobia? Research this term and write an article exploring the discrimination British Muslims have encountered, particularly since the terrorist attacks of 11 September 2001 and 7 July 2005.

5. Find out about the murder of Stephen Lawrence and the MacPherson Report which followed that found the police guilty of institutional racism. Why was this such a defining moment in the history of race relations in the UK? You may find that looking at the 'Stephen Lawrence murder timeline' on *The Telegraph* website helpful (www.telegraph.co.uk/news/uknews/crime/9305537/Stephen-Lawrence-murder-timeline.html).

6. One of your friends tells you a racist joke that you feel is inappropriate. You tell them that jokes like that aren't funny, but your friend says you are being overly sensitive and too 'politically correct'; they were only having a laugh! Is there ever a defence for racist jokes? Do you think your friend would have told you the joke if you belonged to the racial group targeted? What do you think is a good response in this situation? Discuss with a partner and then feedback to your class.

7. Imagine that you write an advice column for a magazine. This week, your topic is 'problems in the workplace'. You receive the following letter:

I believe I am being discriminated against at work. I belong to an ethnic minority, and have worked for a small company in my home town for over five years now. Over the years, I have frequently applied for higher positions and promotions, but I am always unsuccessful. A number of white employees at my company have been promoted instead. I have the same qualifications and experience as them, and everyone tells me that I'm very good at my job. I believe I am being discriminated against because of my race, but am very worried that if I make a complaint it will cause difficulties at work. I enjoy my job, and don't want to leave, but don't want to stay stuck in this position. What should I do?

Write a letter in response, advising what could be done in this situation.

8. With a partner, take it in turns to roleplay a situation in which one of you is being discriminated against because of your race. For example, you could roleplay a policeman stopping a young black man or a student making a joke about a classmate who belongs to the traveller community. The discrimination you reenact could be either direct or indirect, conscious or unconscious. How do you feel when you are playing the part of the person who is being discriminated against?

9. Design a poster that is to be displayed around schools explaining the Race Relations Act 1976.

10. 'All Asians are extremely intelligence.' Can this remark be considered racial discrimination? Why or why not?

11. Look at the illustrations throughout this book. Choose one that grabs your attention. Write a summary analysing what the illustration shows and the impression it makes on you. How does this image reflect the ideas of the article it accompanies?

12. Do you think white people suffer from discrimination in the UK? Discuss this as a group.

13. Using PowerPoint, create a presentation exploring your own background. In the presentation talk about your connection to other countries and cultures. For example, if your parents are from another country you could explore your ties to that culture, or think about any other countries you have visited that may have had an influence on you. Use visual aids such as maps and photographs in your presentation.

ouse, racist 13
la v Employment Service (2002) 2
nisetti v Tokyo-Mitsubushi 2
nti-Muslim hate crime *see* Islamophobia
ttacks, racial 13–15

arristers, ethnic minorities 12
BC v Souster (2001) 1
enign ignorance 28
lack students 19–20
lacking up' 34
ritish National Party (BNP) 37
ullying, racist 16

adbury, accused of racist advertising 29
ampbell, Naomi 29
asual racism 29–30
riminal justice system and ethnic minorities 9, 10

irect discrimination 1–2
against Gypsies and Travellers 22

ast Europeans as victims of racism 32
ducation
and ethnic minorities 10
higher education 10, 19–20
and racism 15, 16
mployment
discriminatory recruitment practices 20
employment prospects for black students 19–20
ethnic pay gap 18
ethnic minorities 10–11
ntertainment industry and ethnic minorities 12
thnic minorities
discrimination in job recruitment 20
life in Britain 6–12
thnic pay gap 18
thnicity and perceptions of racial prejudice 4

erdinand, Anton 38
erdinand, Rio 36, 38
ootball
'anti-Semitic' chanting 39
and ethnic minorities 12
and racism 9, 12, 13, 15, 25, 38
ee speech versus political correctness 35–7

CSE performance, ethnic minorities 10
overnment members from ethnic minorities 11
raffiti, racist 14
riffin, Nick 37
ypsies and Travellers 21–2
Scotland 22

arassment 2–3
igher education 10, 19–20
ungarian immigrants 32

nitations and mockery as indirect racism 28
direct discrimination 2
against Gypsies and Travellers 22
direct racism 28
tegration 17
lamophobia
and the media 23–4
in schools 15

jobs *see* employment
jokes and banter as indirect racism 28
judicial system
ethnic minorities in legal profession 11–12
treatment of ethnic minorities 9–10

law and racial discrimination 1–3, 16
legal profession and ethnic minorities 11–12

media
coverage of Scottish Gypsy Travellers 22
employment of ethnic minorities 11
and Islamophobia 23–4
Metropolitan Police 26
migrants
East Europeans 32
integration 17
mockery as indirect racism 28
MPs from ethnic minorities 11
Muamba, Fabrice 31
Muslims
media portrayal 23–4
as victims of attacks 14
see also Islamophobia

online racism 31

Parliament, ethnic minority members 11
pay gap 18
perceptions of racial prejudice 3–5
police 10, 26–7
political correctness versus free speech 35–7
prejudice *see* racial prejudice

Race Relations Act 1–3, 16
and Gypsies and Travellers 21
racial abuse, Spurs football club 39
racial discrimination 8–12
definitions 1–3
racial prejudice
experiences of 6–8
in football 9, 12, 13, 15, 25, 38
perceptions of 3–5
by police 26–7
prevalence 33
as priority over Islamophobia 25
in schools 15, 16
racial violence 13–15
racism *see* racial prejudice
racist bullying in schools 16
recruitment, discriminatory 20
refusal to engage 28
Romanian immigrants 32

schools and racism 15, 16
Scottish Gypsy Travellers 22
social networking sites 31
sport
and ethnic minorities 12
see also football

Spurs football club, 'anti-Semitic' chants 39
stereotyping of black people 34
street attacks 15
students, black 19–20

teachers, racist bullying 16
Terry, John 38
Tottenham Hotspurs, 'anti-Semitic' chants 39
Travellers 21–2
Twitter 31

unemployment, ethnic minorities 10–11
universities
    black students 19–20
    and ethnic minorities 10

vandalism, racist 14
victimisation 2

wages, ethnic pay gap 18
workers, attacks on 14

Acknowledgements

The publisher is grateful for permission to reproduce the following material.

While every care has been taken to trace and acknowledge copyright, the publisher tenders its apology for an accidental infringement or where copyright has proved untraceable. The publisher would be pleased to come to a suitable arrangement in any such case with the rightful owner.

Chapter One: Racial discrimination

What is race discrimination? © Equality and Human Rights Commission 2012, *Racial prejudice* © Crown copyright 2011, *Growing up with racism in Britain* © Socialist Review, *Race in Britain 2012: Has life changed for ethnic minorities?* © The Independent, *Spotlight on racial violence: January – June 2012* © Institute of Race Relations 2012, *Islamophobia filtering into classrooms* © Awaaz, *Racism in the classroom* © About Equal Opportunities 2000-2012, *Integration in England today* © Crown copyright 2012, *White people paid more and ethnic pay gap widening* © 2012 Institute for Social & Economic Research, *Race to the top: the experiences of black students in higher education* © 2012 Elevation Networks, *A test for racial discrimination, findings* © NatCen, *Racism and discrimination against gypsies and travellers* © Friends Families and Travellers, *Caught in the headlines* © Amnesty International, 1 Euston Street, London WC1 0DW, United Kingdom.

Chapter Two: Debating discrimination

Time to hold the media to account for Islamophobia © 2012 AOL (UK) Limited, *Prioritise the right battle first: not Islamophobia, but racism* © 1st ethical 2012, *Met chief: 'I can't be sure we're not institutionally racist'* © 2012 Brixton Blog, *Police racism: 293 cases, five dismissals* © Channel 4 News 2012, *Confronting indirect racism* © About Equal Opportunities 2000-2012, *Can you excuse casual racism?* © GV Media Group Ltd, *Online racism* © FindLawUK, *Jail for student in Muamba Twitter race rant a perversion of justice* © 1997-2012 Index on Censorship, *Are East Europeans victims of racism in the UK?* © University of Bristol 2012, *One in three Brits admits they are racist* © 2012 OnePoll, *Blackness is not a costume* © StudentJournals.co.uk, *Free speech: Are we getting the balance right?* © 2000-2012 YouGov plc, *A message from British National Party leader Nick Griffin MEP* © 2012 British National Party, *Racism kicked out of football? Not yet* © Guardian News & Media Ltd 2012, *Tottenham defend fans over Society of Black Lawyers threat* © 2012 AOL (UK) Limited.

Illustrations:

Pages 21, 30 : Don Hatcher; pages 18, 38: Angelo Madrid; pages 9, 33: Simon Kneebone.

Images:

Cover and page 6 © Jason Doiy Photography, page 3 © Moon Ape Media, page 14 © bamlou, page 24 © Cara Acred; page 21 © Piotr Lewandowski, pages 26 and 27 © Kashfi Halford, page 32 © Rachel Titiriga, page 39 © Tjanze.

Additional acknowledgements:

Editorial on behalf of Independence Educational Publishers by Cara Acred.

With thanks to the Independence team: Mary Chapman, Sandra Dennis, Christina Hughes, Jackie Staines and Jan Sunderland.

Cara Acred

Cambridge, January 2013